Standing Between
the Gates of Heaven
the Precipice of Hell

A doctor's experience with the afterlife

Theodore Morrison Homa MD

Special thanks to Christine Dugandzic, Robert Maniello MD, and Kathleen D Homa
for their efforts editing this book.

Theodore Morrison Homa M.D. is also the author of "Archimedes'Claw"
The epic novel of one man's journey back through time and his
encounter with mankind's greatest mystery.

"Standing Between the Gates of Heaven and the Precipice of Hell"

Available through Amazon.com and other retailers.

ISBN: 1477599649
ISBN-13: 9781477599648

Preface

I am a soldier trained professionally to do battle with Death. My art and my skills honed to obsessive compulsive fault in the contest against the will of nature that drains us all to our last breath. In our battle against the entropy of existence fought hard by each of us, I have been groomed by human traditions in scientific method and evidence as a mercenary for hire to assist humanity against the inevitable. I am a doctor of medicine.

Throughout my career I have heard with my own ears stories recounted by patients who have been to and beyond the edge of death and come back to tell about it. They all come back changed and convinced that there is indeed an afterlife and a supreme being. Never have I met a patient equipped with the weapon of scientific detachment commonly used by the warriors against death with whom I share my profession. The weapon needed to shield the doctor from the desperate burden of the knowledge that he can never really win this battle but only slow down and put off momentarily the time when death overcomes all heroics and entropy wins.

To this end I have placed pen to paper to share with you my journey to the other side and the lessons learned there. In telling my story I must relate the details of my inner self, my feelings, my fears, who I am and where I have been and perhaps in the telling of the story I can reach out of the scientific world in which I was trained and explain the spiritual world in which we are destined to exist.

It is said of most medical doctors that they train in their profession for altruistic reasons, fame and fortune, or to fulfill the expectations of their parents. There is another reason. It is so wrapped in the cloak of being human and is often overlooked. That reason is to become armed in a vain attempt to cheat death. That I am sure was one of my most personal causes in the quest for mastering medical science. Doctors essentially are human beings that die just like their patients die.

For 12 years before my heart stopped I fought death every day. I used my mind, my skill, my ability to deny, that I was even in the battle to wage constant war against a relentlessly failing heart. I depended on other hired mercenaries whose skills exceeded mine. The war room was the cardiologist's office and the additional weapons were the latest advances in the treatment of congestive heart failure.

When the end came I was able to recognize it approaching and made detachment itself the weapon of choice to use as I rode into the Valley of Death. It did not interrupt the pain or the suffering for me or my loved ones, but the aspect of trying to understand the process from my analytical point of view was as important to me in dying as it was in my professional efforts on behalf of the many patients whose deaths I had delayed for at least some time. Philosophically, we all share the knowledge that in the secular measurable world we have time.

Many have the faith that there is an eternity. Few are lucky enough to be convinced!

When the moment came for me I was laying on a procedure table aware of the doctors efforts to continue to do battle on my behalf. The world of bright lights and excited voices faded in and then went out like the turning of a switch. I experienced the pain of physical life tearing away from my soul and I knew I was dead.

There I found myself dancing as it were on the head of eternity's pin enclosed in a great grey cryptogenic fog the apparent purpose of which was obfuscation. There I felt surrounded by enormous and ancient power delicately limitless, commanding authority, most inescapable surrounded me. It was there that I knew God existed without question.

The following story is written to explain how I got there and how I got back but, most of all how much I have changed during a life long spiritual journey.

Part 1

In the Path of Thomas the Apostle

Chapter 1

Foundations of Faith

When I first got the call to write this book I was sure it was supposed to be about suffering, death, afterlife experience, and recovery of body and soul. I thought I knew where to begin. I was wrong about that and had a sleepless night until I listened to what I sincerely believed was the "voice" of the Holy Spirit and got out of bed in the middle of the night to take notes. It wasn't a voice in the sense of the human experience of voice, but certainly a communication to my inner spirit that would not let me rest until I changed the content of the history that I will recount to you and it was not until I had written the notes, so that I would recall the exact sense of the message I was getting, that I could find the peace to go back to my sleep.

I started my education in Our Lady of Fatima grade school in Scarsdale, New York. I spent 8 years there and graduated in 1959. The first 5 years were with the same teacher, a remarkable nun named Sister Mary Daniel. Her baptized name was Margaret Shannon. She gave me and my fellow classmates a strong foundation in the Catholic faith. Every school day started with Prayers, Patriotism (We stood arm crossed across our chest and Pledged Allegiance to The Flag of the United States of America), and following this we had our first class of the day which was a lesson about the catechism reading, from the Bible, stories about angels especially guardian angels, original sin, the saints and their lives and anecdotes about sister's life and vocation as a nun laced with an occasional appeal to personal discernment about a religious vocation.

The people that shared this experience are still my friends today and we have at this writing even experienced a 50th reunion, for our class of 59., Other nuns worthy of mention here are Sister Rose Anita who taught us music, Sister Ann Gregory who taught all of us art or at least for the untalented an appreciation of art. Sister Sylvester our sixth grade teacher who was a math expert and knew how to push the button that sent me in the direction of science as a career, Sister Patricia Claire focused us on grammar, proper use of the English language, and was our seventh grade teacher, Sister Genevieve who prepared us in eighth grade for the tough years ahead as teenagers and high school. Another nun to mention, Sister Mary Patrick was a sweet and delicate woman who inspired us all with her struggle with multiple sclerosis and her life in a wheelchair.

High school was a different experience for our group as we all went our separate ways. I went to Archbishop Stepinac H.S. in White Plains, New York. The format there was similar but the environment was all male students, Brothers and Priests as teachers. The Catholic religion and Christian point of view was the center of my high school experience and of course the usual challenging subjects in a typical high school curriculum. I personally benefited by the exposure to an advanced placement English literature class and four years of Latin, but I digress as that is another story to be told elsewhere.

College was an easy choice for me. I went with Fordham College so that I could have a car and a New York City kind of life. The secular appeal was overwhelming in spite of the Jesuits I began to lose focus on my Catholic roots and strong beliefs but never gave up on the Philosophy, which was diverse and my minor in college.

Jesuit medical school was not a choice, it just happened to be the first letter of acceptance demanding an immediate reply with a $250.00 check to hold a place. My father was not a rich man and I was not a gambler then.

I enrolled in St. Louis University School of Medicine and after four years there I completed my transition from Catechism Catholic to free thinker and became at best a cultural Catholic, an agnostic and at times an atheist. It is upon this background that my story really begins.

Chapter 2
Denial

Peter denied Christ three times. When he realized what he had done he wept uncontrollably.

I have denied Christ many more times than that, during my life as an agnostic. I did not weep about this for almost three decades.

The secular world and secular progressivism had an appeal to me and I enjoyed living my life by a set of rules that I could pick and choose from a menu as if in a restaurant. Do not misunderstand me. I had a set of values based on the law, science, family, business, friendship, loyalty, and the understanding of that which the great philosophers of history and the modern philosophers of the sixties and seventies have spoken about and written about prolifically. I embraced the philosophy that if something did not harm others it was justifiably correct behavior. My politics were always conservative but not religious conservative. They were more based on the disdain for altruism for altruisms sake expressed in the writings of Ayn Rand. Rand was certain that the proper perspective on life and politics was to be founded upon self-love and personal interest. He believed that good would result from that and that economic success would as well and equated both.

I was most interested in the altruistic goals of helping others with my medical skills, which I honed obsessively to perfection. I knew intrinsically this would lead to wealth and position and most of all respect of my friends and community. I never cheated on time or commitment to the oath I took when I graduated from medical school. Patients flocked to my office and I was successful overnight. I threw myself into work and began to accumulate all the wealth and position and praise that I wanted.

I loved my family and there was never enough time for them because of the way I had immersed myself in the rushing river of life. My wife means the world to me and so do my children. At her demand I attended Mass on Sunday and participated in physical presence only to give, what she demanded would be, a good example to the children. While they prayed I would muse and worry about business and overhead and investments. My pager went off frequently and took me for a needed break from the tedium I perceived was sitting through the Sunday Mass with long meaningless readings, music, and sermons. The priests that I admired then were those that were not "preachy", long winded and were a good challenge on the golf course. My favorite part of Sundays was playing golf at the country club and meeting my family in the grill room for cocktails and dinner. When the season would change and the weather was colder, Sundays with "Meet the Press" blaring from the TV was followed by football, usually the Chicago Bears.

I was never a person who suffered lightly abuse of women or children. I was chivalrous to a fault. I never stole or told lies. I never broke my marriage vows.

I did my share of cursing and swearing. Using God's name in vain was the only time I used it. I publicly honored my father and my mother but privately did not respect my mother and feared my father until I was mature enough to call him my friend, a status my mother never completely shared with me. I coveted a lot and it drove me to work harder. I loved my brother. I was jealous of and misunderstood my sister as the late in life child of my parents, but I did not hold that against her.

I was not opposed to abortion. I was pro death penalty; my attitude was "fry them they earned it". War was a problem for me as I was a product of the sixties but also had a conservative streak and was what I considered a patriot. I certainly did not appreciate being involved with the military at the time of the Vietnam War, but was conflicted about it as well politically I believed someone had to fight the threat of communism. I did not have the avid interest in history that I do now.

While in the Navy, I was a medical officer attached to a Marine Corps air station in Iwakuni, Japan. I met my best friend there and we are best friends to this day. Benn is an African American, he was an atheist, and he had the shade of being a Black Panther politically. We bonded because of our mutual love for practicing good medicine and spent the rest of the time arguing about race, politics and religion. We were also avid boxing fans.

After life in the military I had the world by the tail until the day my brother died. I used God's name then and not in a prayerful way.

In 1984 my grade school class had a reunion. I remade the acquaintance of the treasured friends of my youth. We all came there with a purpose and I will not guess what was in every individual's mind. The thing about it, that was not so good for me was that I was not proud to be Catholic then and had to hide that from my friends because of my pride.

In October of 2009 I attended the fiftieth reunion of Our Lady of Fatima Grammar School. At that time, I had hoped to tell my old friends about the spiritual journey I have taken in the last fifty years and share with them my plunge into agnosticism and my rescue back into faith in God. Unfortunately, a good percentage of them had gone in the direction the secular world first took me and haven't made the leap of Faith required of them to come back to their spiritual roots. The most meaningful thing I can give to them is that which I learned when I died and was resuscitated. It was during that moment that I stood between the gates of Heaven and the precipice of Hell that granted me an insight that few living men have experienced. I discovered unequivocally that, faith in the Lord and his plan for eternal life is justified.

Chapter 3

The Road to Damascus

During the Christmas season of 1986 I received a Christmas card from Christine Dugandzic an old, close friend from grammar school. In it was a letter informing me that she wanted me to know about a place in Yugoslavia, where the Virgin Mary was supposedly having apparitions to a group of young visionaries. It was a town called Medjugorje. I scoffed at the content of the letter, being skeptical of anything religious. I discarded the letter and the card. I considered calling her and teasing her about such foolishness and chose to ignore her rather than have a confrontation over my differing opinion.

She phoned me! I went off into something of a tirade about the content of her letter and told her I could not be part of such religious fantasy of some superstitious kids from Croatia. I stepped it up in intensity, called it cultism and continued a tirade much out of character for me and most unchivalrous.

I was in retrospect, Paul on the road to Damascus, and I was persecuting her and she knew it. I in fact brought her to tears before I stopped and apologized. I informed her calmly, that this kind of stuff was no longer a part of my belief system, if I had one at all. We talked for a while and she calmly asked if I would consider looking at some video tapes on the subject. Guilt ridden with how badly I had treated her, I consented to have her mail them to me and gave some shallow promise that I would review them. We said goodbye and had no further contact until late that summer.

It was summer and baseball season. I had precious little time for me! When the season came I made more time, time to watch my son Teddy play baseball. He was good at it and I rarely missed a game. He had a temper like mine and a drive like mine but ability at sports, especially baseball that I never had. I dreamed of a career in baseball for him, even if he didn't! I took pride in his fastball and more pride in his up and inside slider. He was a "pull" hitter and could slam a ball over the leftfield fence almost at will.

When he did not have a game I would spend the rest of my time working, golfing, and all my other spare time watching baseball on television. My passion for baseball was all consuming. I worshiped at its temple. Like Paul, I would passionately oppose any effort of anyone who would come between me and my form of adoration.

The moment came one day when my in-laws came up to Chicago for the weekend to see one of Teddy's baseball games. The game ended of course, with a victory for our side and we came home to enjoy the afternoon. For me that meant watching the Yankees play the Red Sox on large screen television with surround sound set at stadium mode. It was always like being there for Armageddon. It was always for me, the classic battle between good and evil. In those days the Yankees were the angels and the Red Sox were the demons, the only demons I believed in.

Kathy, my dear wife and my mother-in –law staked out the opposite ends of the couch, where I was watching the demons beat up the angels, and began a conversation across the couch, with me trapped in the middle. The score was getting worse for my Yankees and I could not hear the announcers discuss the game above the constant static of their conversation. I despaired at any further attempts at happiness at that moment and sought my revenge on the distracters. I went to the cabinet where I had hidden the videos that Christine had sent me. My intent was to trap the real believers in the trappings of the Virgin Mary fantasy and end the din in the den. I placed the first tape in the VCR and sat down and waited for them to watch it and watched the video myself with a jaundiced eye.

There appeared on the big screen an unlikely character named Mother Angelica. She reminded me of an old Sister Mary Daniel. She sat at a desk peering thru her spectacles at a middle aged woman named Rita Klaus. The subsequent interview transfixed me. Rita Klaus told the story of her crippling ordeal with multiple sclerosis. She had been unable to walk and had developed painful flexion contractures of her legs at the knees. These contractures occur in patients with end stage multiple sclerosis. The tendons in their hamstrings shorten from lack of nerve function to the muscle in the thigh, a result of the multiple sclerosis. Soon these tendons become so contracted that the tendons and hamstring muscles become painful. The pain is excruciating and there is no way to stop it unless the tendons are cut surgically. Once cut, the tendons become even shorter and the prospect of walking ever again is over. Since there is no future possibility of walking for the patient involved this procedure is reserved for only the most hopeless of cases.

Ms. Klaus continued to tell her story that included a devotion to Our Lady of Medjugorje. I don't recall how she got involved in that because that did not interest me at the moment. She went on about the fact that one day she was getting out of her car that had special equipment for her to enable her to drive by hand controls. She fell to the ground and was stuck there, with no neighbors around to notice her and give her a helping hand. She prayed for some help to come.

She invoked the Virgin Mary as Our Lady of Medugorje to intercede for her.

Suddenly, she felt or heard a message from the Virgin Mary to get up and walk on her own. She attempted this and to her surprise she was able to get up and walk. Not only could she walk but she looked carefully at her legs and they were whole again with tendons intact. She claimed it miraculous!

I was impressed and unable to explain it .I did some research into Rita Klaus and discovered that this story was in fact true. I was more than just intrigued. My curiosity about Medjugorje was piqued. I could not let it drop there; I had to see for myself. In Rita Klaus, I had seen the impossible! To quote Acts9: 1-7 "So that you may see again". I got on the telephone, relentlessly tracked down Christine and finding her asked, "How quickly can you help me get to Medjugorje?"

Chapter 4

The Zovko Connection

The telephone conversation with Christine went on for an hour. This time I listened attentively I did inquire of Chris how she became aware of this phenomenon in Bosnia-Herzegovina. She recounted to me the story of a promise she made to her father when she was young and he was on his death bed. The promise was that if she ever learned of an apparition involving the Blessed Virgin Mary she would make a pilgrimage there to pray for his soul.

Her life went on and she ultimately met and fell in love with a man named Ray Dugandzic whose family was rooted in Medjugorje. I marveled at such a coincidence. When Mary started to appear there she was one of the first people to hear the news because of this relationship with her husband Ray.

I listened as she told me about the Zovko family and the friendship that blossomed from their efforts to spread the word in Arizona about Medugorje.

Chris explained to me that she was sure that through her connections with the Zovko's and others that she would be able to find a place for me to stay without the need for me to wait for a tour or organized pilgrimage. I was also in a hurry and had a limited time frame to go there and come back because of my all consuming need to be at work. She patiently listened to me express my needs about traveling there and promised to get back to me after making a few phone calls.

It was my plan for travel, that I would go on a personal pilgrimage there over the Labor Day weekend. It was Christine's turn to scoff at me and I took it like a man, but got the point never the less.

I used the reference to pilgrimage above and need to point out here that that word was not really an adequate description of my intent. I still was not a confirmed believer. Much has changed since then!

Hardly a day passed when Christine called me back with a full set of plans that fit my agenda. I will address this later as the story unfolds.

The difficult question answered, the harder questions came next from Chris. "Do you still remember how to pray the Rosary?" My answer was no. "Do you remember the Stations of the Cross?" Again I said no. "Do you have any references you can use for these and other prayers?" No again. "Then if you don't mind I will send you what you are going to need, as well as some literature about Our Lady of Medjugorje and an author you need to read named Wayne Weible".

Christine had found a space in the home of Stipe Zovko for that particular weekend and a driver who would help me get from Dubrovnik to Medjugorje. I had to do the rest.

I immediately got on the phone and made reservations for a weekend in Yugoslavia and my very first trip to Europe. I marveled at this peculiar departure from my plans to make

Paris the goal of my first European adventure. The fact that I would only need a back pack, jeans, extra toilet paper and a flashlight were also not part of my dream trip to Europe.

Christine's promised prayer books and literature arrived in the nick of time for my departure; so did a phone call from Andy Zovko who introduced himself as my resource on Medjugorje. Mr. Zovko placed himself at my disposal for any questions I might have regarding my trip to there and told me I would be staying at his brother's home which had been converted from farm house to an inn for pilgrims.

I did not know it at the time that this kind man traveled about running prayer groups and healing services for anyone who would come. He drew large crowds in the Chicago metropolitan area and had claimed several healings .This was the first of many conversations I was to have with him. He recounted the names of the individual visionaries to me. He told me that he had arranged personally for me to have a driver for travel to and from the airport in Dubrovnik and that after my return he wanted me to meet with him.

Chapter 5

On The "Road" Again

I packed everything I thought I would need into a back pack, hesitating as I tried to find room for the prayer manuals Christine had sent. I wondered if I would really find them useful or were they unnecessary weight. I packed them as instructed, one doesn't betray a promise to Christine twice I thought.

I was wearing jeans and a golf shirt. I brought a light weight wind breaker and only canvas walking shoes on my feet. This was my first trip to Europe and my wardrobe was more suited to a camping trip in Wisconsin. But, I was following the protocol discussed with Chris. My daughter Natalie handed me her rosary just as we went out the door and I casually tucked it into my jeans pocket.

My wife drove to the airport through afternoon rush hour traffic in the Chicago suburbs. The highway had the usual number of erratic rush hour drivers and I welcomed the safety of the Jeep SUV, especially when I was the passenger. I was supposed to be at the airport a full two hours before an international flight. I was irritated by the inconvenience of it all. Nine–eleven had not occurred yet. I didn't appreciate how easy it was to travel then compared to today. Kathy kissed me goodbye and good luck at the drop-off point for American Airlines and I grabbed my stuff and proceeded to the check in counter for the 7 PM flight to Frankfort, Germany. I presented my ticket to the clerk and she gave me a nasty glance when I told her I had only a carry-on back pack. I was not young enough to be a student, neither of us knew what a terrorist was then and I supposed that she thought I was a starving and soon to be odiferous artist of sorts. She gave me my boarding pass and I was lucky to have a window seat assigned for the flight out so after a few double martinis I could fall asleep for the rest of the flight and not fear that I would lean all over some stranger in coach if I slept.

I boarded the plane on time and we taxied down the smooth O'Hare runway and lifted off one minute late. An hour later I had finished my second martini and declined dinner and leaned into the window for a 6 hour nap. Half way thru the flight I needed another martini to continue the nap but service was good and the liquor was free. I was awake for the last hour of the trip and watched the European landscape go by as we flew toward Frankfort. The bell rang, the steward announced our impending touchdown and shortly I was looking out an airplane window at buildings and equipment that looked surprisingly like that at O'Hare Airport. I made note that Germany was not as exotic as I had thought it would be.

I deplaned into a very different world. Armed guards stationed everywhere. There were two lines for entrance to the German country one for citizens and the other for foreign nationals. The second line was clearly for me. I showed my passport after a half hour in line, had nothing to declare at customs and proceeded into the terminal.

There were thousands of people milling about in front of a large black information board that demonstrated flight numbers, airlines and destinations all at once. The board would clatter loudly as the information changed and time went on. I analyzed the information system and after a few minutes was able to locate my next flight to Dubrovnik, Yugoslavia. To my immediate dismay I learned I would be 4 hours late. There went my ride! No taxi driver, in his right mind would wait that long for a passenger.

I looked about and discovered sleeping benches scattered throughout the terminal, an accommodation that was both welcome and new to me as a traveler without European experience. I found the Admiral's club and took a quick shower and sought out a bench near the clacking information board. I spent the next four hours awake due to the clacking and worried that the schedule would change and I would miss it.

The time finally came for my flight to depart and I boarded it and found a seat on the aisle of a Pan American jet that carried two rows of double seats. Our flight would have one stop at Budapest, Hungary before final arrival at Dubrovnik. Our layover at Budapest was remarkable in that we stayed on the tarmac never approaching a gate. Only three passengers got off and one got on via a stairway that rolled up to the airplane and while this was happening we all had to show our papers to an acne-faced, uniformed kid with a rifle. Hungary was still in transition from the fall of the Soviet Empire.

The soldier was the last to deplane and we lifted off again for our final destination. Not an hour later we landed in Dubrovnik. After deplaning by way of a stairway on wheels we paraded two by two to the passport check. The clerk examined my passport giving it close scrutiny. He looked me in the eye and with half a smile asked me if I had ever been to a communist country before. My answer seemed to startle him, when I said, "it depends on whether you think Massachusetts is a communist country or not!" I don't think he caught the humor in that, but he passed me thru and nobody at customs wanted to look in my back pack.

My big concern now was to find a taxi and negotiate a ride to Medjugorje in a language I couldn't speak or understand. While I was standing there a fellow with a handmade sign approached me. My name was on his sign below his. His name was Pero Dugandzic and I was really astounded. Not only was the taxi driver waiting for me but he had the same last name as the person who convinced me to go on the trip!

Pero showed me to his old beige stick-shift Mercedes Benz taxi and we were off to Medjugorje. Pero's English skills were more than I hoped for and he led a tour as we drove through some of the most beautiful countryside I have seen. It was much like California wine country with old European architecture. The roads however left much to be desired, especially those that hugged the steep precipice of some of the small mountains along the edge of the Adriatic Sea. They were narrow and barely had enough room for one car. Navigating this road as a passenger with an oncoming bus in sight struck a note of terror in my heart. Each time it happened I would hold my breath as Pero skillfully negotiated a path past the bus without allowing more than half the outside tires to leave the road. I also noted the he never used the brakes.

Talking to Pero was enchanting. His pureness of heart glowed through his charm and smile. He was certainly the most considerate taxi driver I have ever had the pleasure to meet. He told stories of his home town, Medjugorje. They revealed a place of deep religious conviction and devotion to family and caring for strangers. I felt the peace in him and as we approached driving over one last hill I saw a peaceful valley and heard the sweet sound of the "Ave Maria" being sung by an unseen multitude echoing thru the valley. It was dusk and everyone was at Mass, Pero advised me.

The din of the distant cities and bustling world was silenced by the Peace of this valley. For the second time I was Paul coming to realize there was more to Christianity than I ever imagined.

Mahatma Gandhi once said that "the loudest human voice cannot reach as far and be heard better that the still whisper of the human conscience". I began to recognize the whisper I had ignored for 30 years.

Chapter 6
Schnapps

There simply are no Martinis in Medjugorje! As Pero took my backpack inside the simple farmhouse he introduced me to Stipe Zovko. Stipe rushed outside to greet me and brought a bottle of cloudy liquid and two ordinary glasses. It was a warm night with a gentle breeze. There was a table out in front of the house with several chairs. He indicated that I should sit and began to pour from the bottle. Introducing me to traditional Croatian welcome smiled a semi toothless grin and said "Schnapps" I took the drink and sipped the bittersweet liquor and repeated the word "Schnapps" Stipe took his drink all at once and waited for me to follow suit. Then he poured another round. Then in broken English he gave me a tour of his orchard and farm. I learned that the drink was home made from a fruit on the trees in the orchard.

While we sat there communicating, Pero joined in and advised me that he would be my driver for the entire weekend.

I was now on an organized, but personal pilgrimage. Pero indicated that he would drive me to Mount Krizevac after breakfast which would be served at dawn. Other pilgrims were there at the Zovko inn and farm. They would be back after evening Mass and prayers. We would all have a Croatian supper at 8 PM followed by early retirement to our rooms.

Stipe grinned in approval and poured another round.

The other guest pilgrims arrived all at once in a bus. They had just returned from a day trip to Mostar, the largest city in the vicinity of Medjugorje. There they met with a holy priest named Fr. Jozo. They all seemed to be quite impressed with their experiences so far. Steve Arcenaux from Metarie, Louisiana was the leader and spokesman for the group. We discussed many things about the visionaries, rosaries turning gold, little signs interpreted as miracles rather than coincidence. We also discussed the history of the region, and the geography and the fact that although our hosts were Croatian, Medjugorje was actually in Bosnia-Herzegovina. Yugoslavia was an arbitrary Nation State composed of three old countries with a long history of ethnic friction. It began in 1918 after World War I when the Austro-Hungarian Empire disintegrated. After World War II it became part of the sphere of influence propped up by the Soviet Union and in 1961 Josef Tito critical of East and West became president for life of the Socialist Republic of Yugoslavia. He died in office in 1980, after which ethnic tensions began to boil to the surface.

There was no evidence of ethnic tension in Medjugorje. The citizens had gone beyond that in true Christian love of neighbor. They welcomed strangers into their homes and slept in lofts and barns to allow pilgrims from the entire world to come and see Medjugorje for themselves. It became clear to me that whatever was going on, it must be from God. The people were prayerful, reverent, holy, charitable and loving of their neighbors as well as the pilgrims.

The meal began with a prayer. Steve Arcenaux led grace before the meal. The food was simple and good. Mounds of freshly baked grain bread were a staple. Some pilgrims only took bread and water, explaining to me that they were fasting. The crowning jewel of the meal was Croatian coffee, a concoction of richly brewed coffee and boiled milk and coarsely refined sugar.

One of the pilgrims a Filipino American woman with a Cajun accent told the sad story of her missing luggage, now almost seven days lost. Town's people and pilgrims alike shared their clothing and necessities with her as if she were family! But the suitcase contained a family heirloom. Her mother's rosary, presumed lost forever.

The discussion of this rosary led to rumors of rosaries turning gold but none of my fellow pilgrims had that experience. They had however seen the sun spin and vacillate in the sky, an experience well known to those who knew the history of the approved apparitions of Our Lady of Fatima.

There were 12 places for pilgrims in Stipe Zovko's house. Someone from New Orleans dropped out at the last minute leaving only 11 and a place for me to fill. I began to see more than coincidence in the number 12!

After supper, exhausted from the day we all retired to our rooms. I fell asleep as my head hit the pillow.

Chapter 7

The Cock Crows

The cock began to crow. I heard three crows until I opened my eyes and looked around the cell. I peered at the screenless open window and saw the crow sitting there on the outside ledge, beckoning me to get out of bed and start my day. I dragged my body out of bed still sleepy and the crow continued until I was on my feet and then abruptly left his perch, presumably to disturb another pilgrim's sleep. Outside the window I could see the grayness of dawn change to the crimson blue of the early morning sky. I smelled rich coffee and shaved in a basin. I took a sponge bath, dressed in a fresh tee shirt put on my only pair of jeans and proceded to the country kitchen where the others were gathering around the table for breakfast. Fresh grain bread was served from the hot oven which was the only source of warmth in the room chasing away the night's chill. When the table was full we said grace before the meal. Steve Arcenaux led the prayers again.

Steppe looked on approvingly while Maria his wife arranged the fresh bread on the table and poured the Croatian coffee.

The bread, I was told was rich in nutrition and was often served alone as a meal for breakfast. It was like serving fresh bran muffins in Chicago. We consumed our meal and shared our plans for the day with one another. My plan involved climbing the mountain with the Cross on the top that stood as a reminder to distant observers that there was a devout Catholic village here in the valley in the midst of this Islamic state of Bosnia-Herzegovina, a member state of the Socialist Republic of Yugoslavia. I looked up from the conversation and saw Pero standing arms crossed on his chest patiently waiting to drive me to Mt. Krizevac. I understood from his body language that I must go then and I excused myself and left the farmhouse to get into the dusty beige Mercedes taxi.

Pero began the tour as we drove to the mountain pointing out various important places in Medjugorje. When we arrived at the foot of the mountain he told me that he would be waiting for me when I came down and that I must be down for evening Mass and prayers at the church of St James. He advised me that the apparitions started in the choir loft before Mass. He also stated that Mary blessed all the people, rosaries and other religious articles that were brought there in time for the apparition. His serious and frank discussion left me hungry for more knowledge. The peace of the Lord began to come to me as quietly as a kitten about to pounce upon me. I took my prayer book out of my back pack. It was tucked in there between several bottles of drinking water I had brought for this occasion. I began my assent up the mountain, thinking about the world I left behind 36 hours before. I followed a well-worn path until approaching a marker which was clearly marked with the Roman numeral 1 and understood that this was the first Station of the Cross.

I opened my book to the Stations of the Cross section and began, not so much as a prayer but a reading of the words with an attempt to remember when I last had done this ritual and what its meaning was.

I continued to climb as the path became rocky and steep I got thirsty. I had just arrived at the fourth station of the cross; the one where Jesus meets his mother Mary. When I got there, there appeared to be a beggar holding a tin cup toward me. He only had one leg and a crutch. As I got closer he appeared to be begging alms and my thoughts were that even here there were "street" people who would use their disability to arouse guilt in you so that you would feel the need to give a donation. I hardly ever caved into this rouse back home in Chicago. I did marvel at how difficult it must have been for a one legged man to climb up, this far, to beg for money. I was resolute as I approached him that I would not fall for this trick. I learned my lessons on the streets of Manhattan well during my "New York kind of life" years! To my utter amazement when I was within arm's length of him he pushed the cup at me and it contained pure cold water. He motioned to me to drink from the cup and I did. I walked away further up the mountain trail my thirst satiated and thinking of how I had prejudged the one legged man. I went back down the trail I had followed to thank him. He was gone without a trace. I went down further and saw no sight of anyone! I climbed back up to the fourth station opened my prayer book and this time it was not just reading but true prayer.

I stayed there a long time reflecting on why I had come this far to learn this lesson. I recalled Sister Mary Daniel at Our Lady of Fatima grammar school. I remembered the parable of the rich man and the leper. She used to tell us about it during religion class. She even had a poster that she put on an easel showing this poor leper waiting outside the rich man's door. Dogs were licking his wounds. He was hungry, just waiting in hope that he would be given the scraps from the rich man's table. We were told that beyond that door, the rich man lived in luxury oblivious to the suffering of the leper. However he did consent to give Lazarus the leper some table scraps. As the parable goes on to reveal both Lazarus and the rich man die. Lazarus finds himself at the feast in paradise seated at Abraham's table. Across an abyss the rich man suffers in the heat and flames of hell. He asks Lazarus to give him just a drop of water to cool him in his torment. Lazarus wants to do this but is unable to cross the abyss to get to the rich man. I did not even practice the kindness of the rich man in my life. I would not have given Lazarus table scraps then. My conscience whispered loudly at me and I saw the evils of the path I had followed before I found myself on this path up the mountain. I prayed harder. I asked who that one legged man was that quenched my thirst. Was he just a man? Was he an angel? He disappeared so quickly! Was it Jesus? I did not know. I just knew from that moment my life would never be the same. My curiosity melted away some more and I felt the resurgence of faith. I pondered the Story of the fourth station of the cross. Jesus meets his Mother. What did she think of what they had done to her Son? What did she think of sinners like me, for whom He endured this? What did He think? After a timeless stay at this station I got up with renewed faith and was determined to get to the top of Mount Krizevac.

Chapter 8
On Top of the Mountain

I started up the rocky path again this time determined to get to the top as quickly as I could. At each station of the Cross I tempered my pace by stopping to pray and read the appropriate readings from "The Way of The Cross" the booklet I carried with me. The journey up became timeless and soon I found myself on the top of Mount Krizevac peering at a cross that stood 8.5 meters tall. There were others up there of course, they were from very diverse ethnic and cultural backgrounds. All either prayed reverently or meditated quietly. The top of the mountain was noticeably without the social chatter one normally hears in crowds. The view was spectacular. The air was warm and fresh. The place had an intense feeling of peacefulness. I spent my time there reading and praying. I was aware that a miracle of sorts had occurred in my sudden transformation back to Faith in God. I welcomed this and took joy in it. I saw how I felt in the faces of others who were there in that holy place. I felt a renewed sense of hope. I felt love and understanding for those fellow pilgrims who were strangers to me yet in a close bond with me as a result of our presence there.

I spent time reading about Krizevac. Literally translated it means Cross Mountain. The 8.5 meter tall cross was finished on March 15 1934. It was built by Fr. Bernadin Smoljan and the parishioners of St. James Church. The materials used were carried up the steep mountainside by the parishioners on their backs. The cross was made of reinforced concrete. there is an inscription on the cross that states," To Jesus Christ, the Redeemer of the human race, as a sign of our Faith, Love, and Hope, in memory of the 1900th anniversary of the Passion of Jesus". In the center of the cross they placed a true relic of the authentic Cross of Jesus. This relic was received as a gift from Rome where the larger part of the authentic Cross is kept in the Church of Santa Croce di Gerusalemme`. Ever since, it has been a custom to celebrate Holy Mass at its base on the first Sunday after September 8, in honor of the Triumph of the Cross.

There are many stories about the top of this mountain and miracles that occur there. I for one enjoyed a total release from the tensions and worries of the past and the burdens of the present. It seemed to me that the mountain top was outside of time and the joy of being there was palpable. I now have a kinship with those I meet elsewhere in the world who have shared this same experience. The 34th Psalm line 4 best sums up what it was like; "I sought the Lord and He answered me and delivered me from all my fears"

I broke from my meditations after a long seamless time and discovered it was late afternoon and I reluctantly left the top of Krizevac. Knowing I would not be returning again left me feeling a sense of loss. The travel down the path was much easier than the ascent made that morning. When I got to the base Pero was there as promised with his dusty beige Mercedes taxi and we drove to the center of town where he dropped me off with a set of instructions about how to walk the short distance back to the Zovko house. I walked about the square in front of the St. James Church and first noticed the vendors lined up along the street. Window shopping was never my forte, but I worked my way through each and every kiosk until I found the religious artifacts I sought. A substantial set of rosary beads for my mother and one for myself, a bag of medals with Our Lady of Medjugorje engraved on them as requested by my wife and daughter, and more books and of course post cards. I sat on a wall outside of church awaiting the evening Mass during which the apparitions occurred. The church was massive and cathedral like in its architecture. Although built years ago it seemed right for accommodating the huge crowd that seemed to be assembling in the square. I noticed thousands of birds perching on rooftops and wires all about. They were not singing just waiting as if they realized the presence of heaven's hand in what was about to happen. While I sat there I wrote a postcard to each of my children and my wife with personal messages of fatherly love for the children and husbandly love for my wife. In each card I mentioned the love of God that had reawakened in my soul. At the sound of the church bell the pilgrims were summoned to come into the church. I followed.

Chapter 9

The Miracle of the Sun

I took a seat next to a talkative woman with a New York accent. She made me feel right at home. I could not call it a conversation as I could not get a word in edgeways. She spoke of rosaries turning gold and the sun spinning and vacillating as it did at Fatima when The Virgin Mary appeared there. We were next to a large double door on the western side of the church building with the doors wide open to keep the inside cool. Mass started. The New York woman stopped speaking and I paid attention to the Mass for the first time in years. Wondering what would happen when the apparitions occurred in the choir loft was my only distraction as I kept a tight grip on the religious articles I had purchased outside. I knew now that when Mary came to the visionaries she would bless these articles with a special sort of blessing. I followed the Mass. Just before the consecration the woman from New York tugged my arm and told me to look out the doors at the sun. To my amazement the sun was vacillating in the sky. Spinning in a pinwheel of bright colors that trailed outwards from the center, the sun itself seemed to be breaking the laws of nature. I watched until it stopped. There was a murmur that ran through the church like a wave of awareness as other pilgrims bore witness to the event. It then stopped abruptly. Mass continued, all eyes now focused on the altar during the consecration of the Body and Blood of Jesus from bread and wine. When Communion started I refrained from going up to receive realizing clearly that it was required of me to receive the sacrament of reconciliation first. Mass ended with the usual blessing and the Ave Maria begun once again to echo through the valley as the pilgrims and parishioners alike retreated from St. James Church to their evening destinations. Mine was the open confessionals set up around the perimeter of the church like sentinels. I chose the shortest line. Three hours later after meeting Father Philip Pavich for the first time face to face in the Sacrament of Penance, I walked to the Zovko house in the cool evening. I was at peace with myself for the first time in years and with the Lord as well. It felt even better than I felt on top of the Cross Mountain. Armed with my day's experience to share with others I entered the house. Everyone was assembled at the dinner table patiently waiting for me. Steve Arceneaux led "Grace before Meals" again. Maria Zovko served a delicious meal and we all traded stories. Several demonstrated their now gold rosaries. I felt the envy rise in me for such a treasure and quickly suppressed it. I shared my story about the assent up Krizevac and the spinning of the sun. Most of them had witnessed the miracle of the sun that same day. The young Filipino woman whose luggage was lost still had heard nothing about it. We all prayed together that evening that it would be found soon. The meal ended with a prayer and we retired to our bedchambers for the night.

Chapter 10
The Dawn of Doubt

That night was a restless night for me. The excitement of the day and the peace of the Lord faded into a troubling nagging sensation that kept me tossing and turning. There was no need for the cock to crow at me in the morning. I was up before that with a headache and a realization that I was obsessed by feelings of doubt. How could that be after witnessing miracles with my own eyes and making peace with the Lord after 3 decades of unholy war? I should be certain by now! The things that I saw, the gold rosaries that I held in my hand and examined carefully should be enough to shore up belief in even the hardest of hearts. I bathed and shaved and presented myself for breakfast quietly. I did not interact with the others. After another breakfast of grain bread and rich Croatian coffee, I met a substitute driver. I felt worse and abandoned by Pero. I do not remember the name of the new driver. He told me Pero would be back from an emergency trip to Mostar the next day. Today we would go to Apparition Hill. Once there I would follow the crowds to the location of the first apparitions on a hillside pasture. The walk home to the house would be longer, but I would be with many more pilgrims who would know the way back to town. From there I could easily find the Zovko house.

The hill was not steep; the path broad and rocky. At some distance from the path was un-trodden pasture. Along the path and littering the hillside were tens of thousands of prayer petitions. They were dropped there, some held in place by a rock or a spike or even affixed to small cross like shrines. *Wishes Crucified,* was what struck my mind about these as I continued to struggle with my accelerating feeling of doubt. The whole place was depressing me and I felt waves of apathy about the prayers of pilgrims left on the crowded but lonely hillside. I got to the site of the first apparition and felt empty! Not what I expected. I thought about all those prayers for presumably desperate situations. Does God really listen to them? Does He ever answer them? Is He real? Am I just caught up in group hysteria? How could I know for sure? Thomas the apostle did not believe his most trusted friends about the Resurrection of Christ. He had to put his hand into the wounds to believe. Was that just a fable too?

I prayed there from my heart. I prayed for more knowledge. I prayed and asked for God to answer all of those petitions scattered around the hillside in chaos by the wind and trampled under the feet of marching pilgrims. Marching to what end was the question that echoed thru my mind and my very soul. I picked up a heavy stone and put it in my back pack like a zombie. It was an errand for my wife, to bring back a rock from the Hill of Apparitions. The rock was heavy, so was my heart.

I departed quickly and had plenty of time that afternoon to distract myself from the experience of the morning and the nagging from within. I had a conversation with a man dressed in tennis gear who was there to play tennis with a rich friend who had a resort home in the quiet countryside. He complained that things had changed in the valley since this had all started. I challenged him with a question. "Do you believe that Mary is appearing here?" His response was that he did not really believe it and it was not his concern.

I left him and came upon the square in front of St. James' Church. I found the same stone wall I sat upon the day before. The plan came to me. I would have one more conversation with Father Pavich and discuss my feelings of doubt with him. He would be able to help me. He certainly had a deep understanding of me when he heard my life confession the night before. I inquired at the rectory if he were there and was told no. I spent hours watching who came and went from the Church and rectory in hope of finding Father Pavich and asking my question. As time for Mass approached I despaired of being able to get an answer from Father Pavich. The church bells announced the evening Mass. I entered the church and found a pew. It was close to the front. Shortly an entourage of altar servers and priests paraded onto the altar. Among them and garbed as the Main celebrant of the Mass was Father Philip Pavich! I don't to this day know how I could have missed seeing him enter the rectory or church during my stakeout.

As Mass proceeded thru the Gospel it became apparent that Fr. Pavich would deliver the homily. As he began to speak he said "Today I would like to talk to you about doubt"!

Chapter 11

The Chain Reaction

With less than 24 hours left in Yugoslavia there was much to do. The evening before my last day I sat at dinner with my newly acquired friends and listened to all of the good news of their pilgrimage. The missing luggage with the heirloom rosary in it was found and would be there in the morning. All of the pilgrims from New Orleans had seen the sun spin in the sky. Several spoke of meeting the visionaries. The universal favorite was Vicka Ivankovic who seemed the most personable. It was reported that she spent the entire day listening to each and every pilgrim who approached her with questions and petitions, never showing impatience or fatigue. That was my experience the next morning when Pero drove me to her home to meet her. I was the only one in the crowd of pilgrims that she gazed at and listened to, when it became my turn. I handed her a petition from my sister, requesting that God bless her with a child. My sister and her husband Mark had been trying without luck to conceive and remain pregnant for several years. The last day was filled with little errands such as the procurement of more rosaries and religious artifacts for those at home who might want or need them. My plane was to depart from Dubrovnik at 6AM the next morning. The departure time meant there was no time for sleep or late dinner at the Zovko table. The plan was to attend the evening Mass and meet in a field near the church for final goodbyes with my group. We all held hands standing in a circle and took turns leading in a final rosary. After that the young Filipino woman in our group announced the recovery of her luggage and the rosary she could not afford to lose. She passed it around to each of us explaining that when she opened her suitcase the rosary had turned gold. I can bear witness to the fact that the chain was indeed a glistening gold color and looked new compared to the beads worn down by generations of use. I left the group with Pero to begin the trip home, considering the fact that I had come so far in such a short time and how this journey had changed my very soul. I was given a new chance at life, this time spiritual and looked forward to going home to share my new feelings of faith with my family and friends. I did not understand at that time the chain reaction this would cause in my life.

The ride to Dubrovnik was more relaxed as we had time to explore the city and some of its famous buildings. Pero had once again proven himself as an excellent guide. It was late when we got there and we were hungry having missed dinner in Medjugorje. Pero drove about looking for an open restaurant. We thought after many disappointments that it would be a long hungry night when Pero spotted one with an enormous crowd. We parked the taxi and went inside. We had walked in on a wedding party. In the spirit of hospitality

I had felt since arriving in Croatia we were invited to join the party. We ate and drank our fill and after properly thanking our unexpected hosts returned to the taxi and drove to the airport. The doors were locked at 3 AM so Pero waited with me and we napped in the taxi until 5 AM when the terminal was unlocked. I said goodbye to my new friend and entered the terminal with back pack in hand. I checked in first and waited by the gate to board the plane. No delays this time, we lifted off on schedule and were soon in Frankfort. There was a long chain of people waiting to go through the passport check point but other than that the connection was seamless. Once on board I fell asleep and awakened when the steward tapped my shoulder and asked me to fasten my seatbelt to land at Chicago's O'Hare airport. Once again through customs and passport control I was free to walk to the passenger pickup lane where my wife Kathy was waiting for me in the SUV.

I couldn't stop talking all the way home and announced to her that she must go herself to Medjugorje or she couldn't possibly understand me and what transformed me. She protested that she did not need to go but agreed after I persisted, reminding myself of how my friend Christine persevered in her effort to get me to take this journey. We arrived at home and I greeted all my children as if I had not really seen them for years. My first child Natalie asked me for her rosary back and asked if I had used it. I reassured her that I had worn it out! She held it in her hand and exclaimed aloud "Something happened to my rosary." We all looked in amazement as we saw the chain holding the beads together was now gold.

It was in mid- October that I flew to Boston to see the fall colors and to close the summer house for the winter. Kathy was anxious about the trip to Medjugorje because of rumors of impending war between the factions of Yugoslavia as it crumbled into individual ethnic states due to the international political winds of that time. We discussed it at length and I backed off on my insistence that she go, but asked her to pray about it. She never was without her rosary and pulled it out of her purse and retreated into silent prayer while I read a book about history. After about five minutes she shook my arm. She demonstrated a rosary on which the chains connecting the beads she had prayed on had turned gold but those yet to be prayed were still the color of steel wire. As she prayed more the chain continued its transformation before our eyes. She said to me, "I guess I have my answer."

I will recount to the reader the fact that when we got back from our trip Kathy found a willing travel companion named Linda and together they planned and carried out a pilgrimage to Medjugorje. With Christine's help they stayed at the Zovko house and Pero was their driver. When they returned home I learned of many miraculous experiences that they both had. Of course Linda's rosary turned gold. They both witnessed the sun spinning. The most impressive thing that happened to them was that they too had a very awful experience climbing apparition hill. It was raining hard and they were muddy and cold. After leaving petitions and photos of loved ones on the hillside they quickly retreated to the warmth and dryness of the Zovko house. Maria, Stipe's wife, greeting them at the door realizing their misery sat them down on a bench and knelt and took off their "walking shoes" and socks. In an instant she plunged the muddy shoes into a bucket of soapy water to clean them. Kathy remembers thinking that this was the beginning of the worst possible trip ever as there was no way to dry the inside of the shoes now and she imagined slogging around with constantly wet walking shoe for several days. Maria ignored the exclamation of "Oh no!" She instead continued to scrub the shoes inside and out. When she was done she put the shoes back on their feet. At that moment not only were the shoes dry but so were their clothes!

Weeks after Kathy's return from Medjugorje we heard from my sister. She was pregnant for the first time! Her first born named Grace was born March 27, 1990; a coincidence or an answer to prayer? Now, I knew the difference.

In the spring of 1990 we went to Cape Cod to visit my parents for Easter. My mother had been praying for my father's conversion back to God for the 50 years they had been married. On the occasion of my return from Medjugorje I had given her a rosary obtained there and blessed by the Virgin Mary during an apparition as well as Fr. Pavich. I had made it my habit of frequently looking at the chain to see if she would be given the favor from God of having it turn to gold. Up until now it never did. On Holy Saturday we visited again. The rosary chain was still the color of steel. On Easter morning mom called very excited. Pop had followed her down the aisle at Mass and received Communion. He had kept secret the fact that during a hospitalization weeks before he had sought out the Catholic chaplain and had gone to confession for the first time in 50 years. We were all elated at the news. After Mass we went to my parent's home for an Easter feast. I went to my mother's bedroom on arrival there to look at the rosary hung in its usual place on her bed post. The chain had transformed to gold! My father died just 3 weeks short of his 79th birthday that same year.

Part 2
After the Change

Chapter 12
Watershed Moments

L ife after returning from Medjugorje had a new focus. Just like Baptism which changes us when it happens to us or when we choose it, spiritual life begins anew. But it is never easy to put down the old life before the awakening we receive from the "water" if we have grown accustomed to it during our less innocent years. Change is always difficult and most people fear change. When your boss calls you into his office you expect the worst, perhaps a termination interview. It is a surprise when it is for a pat on the back or even a raise. We have learned responses and habits which make us comfortable. We even contrive logical arguments to reinforce our old familiar standards and beliefs.

We share one of those moments with David in Scripture. David was a warrior and King. He was a man grown accustomed to habits which might be focused on his own pleasure or comfort and not on his covenant with God. In 2 Samuel 23 15-17 the scriptures speak of David longing for a drink of water from the well by the gate of Bethlehem. When the warriors known as the Three broke through the enemy lines into the camp of the Philistines who occupied Bethlehem and fetched for David a flask of water from this well they brought it to David. He had second thoughts and refused to drink it and poured it out on the ground in tribute to the Lord and to the Three who had risked everything to give it to him. He essentially remembered he had a higher calling than to mere earthly luxury.

Water is the symbol of physical life and also the symbol for spiritual life. Water is a barrier to cross as in the Jews escaping from Egypt and crossing the Nile with the help of God parting the waters. This also became a sign of God's assistance and loyalty to His chosen people. Water can be a threat to physical life, as we see in the storm that suddenly arose in the Sea of Galilee threatening the apostles, until Jesus asleep in the back of the boat was awakened and calmed the sea with a miracle.

Water is an essential requirement for sustaining life. The human body and most other living creatures on this planet are more than 60 to 90% water in content. The living human child as a fetus floats serenely in water inside the womb as it develops. Lack of water can result in death of a living being and in as little as three days for human beings.

Throughout history water on our planet was involved in unique moments in history. Man's capacity to navigate and cross large bodies of water led to new discoveries and new paradigms in the course of human history. The Roman Empire depended on control of merchant routes and naval forces in the Mediterranean Sea. The Romans held their civilization together by the construction of a system of aqueducts that provided water for civilization and agriculture. Columbus discovered the Americas by sailing across the Atlantic Ocean in a primitive fleet of ships. The fortune in gold that supported the Spanish armada was lost in a devastating hurricane at sea, thus altering history and their influence in the Americas. The Mississippi River valley and it's tributaries became the conduit for the commerce that sustained the growth of the United States of America and the development of New Orleans as the largest seaport in the world. Yet as the technology improved to cross great barrier seas we are constantly reminded of the limits placed on us by God's creation. Pride resulted in the building of the unsinkable Titanic. The massive Edmond Fitzgerald floundered at sea and sunk in the Great Lakes giving historical signs or markers to the limits of man. World War I started because of the sinking of the Lusitania. The United States of America was drawn into World War II because of the bombing and sinking of the pacific naval fleet at Pearl Harbor. Wars in Africa have been fought over the rights to control sources of water. Agricultural development requires access to adequate supplies of water.

The great sea port of New Orleans became a site of tremendous loss of life and property, fueling the roots of political change due to the devastating flood from the dikes failing just after Hurricane Katrina struck. The recent tsunami that devastated Japan with massive waves of water, interrupted industry and harmed the entire national economy. The residual threat because of the tsunami still exists in the shutdown of four nuclear power plants and the threat that one could still explode and spread radioactive material throughout the northern hemisphere. Water can be a threat to human civilization due to climate change causing melting polar ice caps and rising sea levels. Water clearly is intimately tied to physical life, spiritual life and death.

* * *

Water poured out from the side of Jesus on the Cross to mark the finality of His crucifixion and physical death.

Life of men, civilizations and history are marked by points in time that I call watershed moments. In the following chapters of part 2 of this book I will share with you those watershed moments of my own personal experience and those of others who are friends in the Lord.

Chapter 13

The Meandering River of Life

L ife of course never follows the exact direction that you imagine that it would go. It is more like a river. A bend here and a bend there, but sooner or later the river and life get to their final destination. So it was with my life after my conversion. I knew where I wanted to go but getting there was a series of meandering bends and some very turbulent waters.

My wife Kathy and I spent the normal amount of time that most parents of teenage children do trying to keep them safe and focused on their goals. With a little persuasion and a lot of hard work we were successful at least in keeping them all in the same boat as ourselves. It was not difficult for us to make the decision that the oldest should go on a pilgrimage to Medjugorje. We had both joined a prayer group and we learned from other members of that group that a Roman Catholic priest named Fr. Ken Roberts was leading tours to

Medjugorje. Our interest peaked in sending Natalie on one of his pilgrimages when we learned more about him on EWTN the same network where I first saw Mother Angelica and Rita Klaus speaking about miracles related to Medjugorje. Fr. Ken Roberts was somewhat a celebrity in the circles of public missions, broadcasts related to Roman Catholic issues, and was also a celebrity author. His most famous publication was "Playboy to Priest". We had no difficulty with our decision based on his solid credentials.

Natalie came back full of the Spirit after her pilgrimage and plotted her course through life with little difficulty. She knew who she was, had self-assurance, good self-esteem and was very intelligent. She was also intent on a career in the classics. She headed off to Holy Cross College and majored in Latin. I was still working 16 hours a day and faced with a prospective $120,000 cost for this degree. I asked her many times and myself more, "How does a degree in Latin prepare one for real life and financial security? Though I was hesitant, I knew that I could trust her instincts and had learned from the new values related to my conversion, to trust in God and not to tell Him my plans for her. She went on to get two master's degrees. The first was from Rutgers University and the second one was tailor made for her at Northwestern University. Her degree from Northwestern was in Teaching Latin to grammar school students! After graduation she was immediately sought after by numerous school systems and landed a plum of a job in the Lake Forest, Illinois grammar school system where she was given the opportunity for not only employment but the authorization to be the designer of their Latin and Classics program. The result was very reassuring to me and more evidence that trusting in the Lord was the right decision to make.

When my daughter Priscilla was a junior in a Catholic high school she was one of the prettiest and most popular girls in the school. She was also rebellious enough to cause Kathy and me some worry! We decided it was time to expose her to a religious pilgrimage but by then the war in Bosnia was intense and the danger of a trip there too much to accept. By this time Pope John Paul II had planned a trip to The United States to celebrate World Youth Day in Denver. As it turned out Fr. Robert's was leading a tour of youths to make a pilgrimage to Denver to see the Pope. We discussed it with Priscilla and she, reluctantly agreed to go.

I remember watching with enthusiasm the events in Denver while John Paul II said Mass. It was a EWTN Broadcast. My thoughts drifted back to that first EWTN broadcast that changed the direction in which my life was flowing. I hoped Priscilla's experience would be of similar benefit to her.

She came home, a remarkably changed person. She was filled with the Spirit and a new zeal for evangelization of the Roman Catholic Church. She took this with her to her Catholic high school and was almost immediately rejected by all of her "friends". This rejection, evolved into persecution and bullying. We were astounded! It seemed that even the teachers who were aware of this process and Priscilla's pain from it, stood by and allowed it to go on. The persecution pushed Priscilla into depression and withdrawal from life. Her grades plummeted and she cried for hours every day. It became burdensome to come home from work at the end of a stressful day and witness her anguish never seeming to stop. I am sure this is one of those watershed events that took its toll on the whole family and ultimately on my own health. I began to assimilate some of her depression. The sadness was profound and inescapable.

One day when another dismal week was over I was looking forward to some good news but there was no change when I got home. I had made plans with Kathy to escape to a local French restaurant for several hours that night. The restaurant was exclusive and reservations had to be planned months in advance.

The phone rang! The voice on the other end was a kind soft, gentle, manly voice with a British accent. It was familiar but foreign at the same time. He asked with the gentleness of an angel "Is Priscilla there?". I asked who was calling; "Its Fr. Ken Roberts" was his reply. I almost dropped the phone!

I ran to get Priscilla, who upon hearing the news brightened with a smile not seen for months and raced to the phone!

Chapter 14

Stilling The Waters

The arrival of Ken Roberts in all of our lives began with that moment. Priscilla's tears crystallized into diamonds in the reflection of her smiling eyes. A great peace came over the family again as God's grace seemed to remove the thorn in her side placed by an angel of Satan. Like Paul, Priscilla and the rest of the family prayed for relief from this time of troubled waters. Like Paul, the message from the Lord was "My grace is sufficient for you, for power is made perfect in weakness". Having understood this message Priscilla got the relief symbolized by the arrival of Ken Roberts and rose from within to become a tower of strength and commitment to the Lord. It was she, not Fr. Ken that led the rest of us out of the desert to the cool refreshing waters of an oasis. At that critical moment she became a leader and a more powerful force for evangelizing than even she had dreamed she would be. Her life began to take a new shape. She put down her ties to old ways and looked forward with great resolve to her next challenge. At the end of her junior year she was accepted as an early admission to Franciscan University without waiting to graduate from high school. By the end of that summer she accomplished getting her GED and enrolled in College with the will and determination to succeed. Her self-esteem was strengthened in God's will. She never looked back again.

We all went to the Rosemont auditorium and listened while the speakers at the mission gave their testimony. Fr. Roberts said the Mass that evening and gave an extraordinary homily. His friends from California found us at a prearranged meeting place when the evening program was completed. We all then departed the grounds with Fr. Ken Roberts among us and went to a restaurant.

I was grateful to the priest for what he had already done for my girls, regarding their spiritual awakening. I was unaccustomed to priests as celebrities and as I sat across the table from Father Ken, I was briefly at a loss for words while others in the large group seemed to pour upon him a flood of attention. I sized up the Priest at a glance and noticed the cigarette constantly dangling from his lip. I listened to the conversation carefully. He was complaining about leg pain. I suddenly realized what I had to offer him in return for the care he had shown to my daughters.

"You look terrible" my voice boomed, at that precise moment all the conversations at the table stopped! Ken looked at me and said "I feel as bad as I look, can you help?" For a few seconds I thought I had planted my foot deeply in my mouth. On his face was a look of concern to match his response to my abrupt statement. I thought to myself how unlikely it would be for me to take such an aggressive stand with a priest, especially one of celebrity. Our discussion continued as others around us resumed their previous conversations. Fr. Ken went on to tell me that when he walked through an airport or ran to catch a taxi during his almost daily travels his right leg would ache enough to stop him in his tracks. This had been going on for several months and was getting worse. He paused to light another cigarette, a practice that was a habit to him and had not yet been banned from restaurants in Illinois.

I asked him when the last time was that he saw his doctor. He informed me that he liked to avoid doctors as he was uncomfortable with illness. I asked how long he had been smoking. He went on to say that he had a pack a day habit going back to his younger days. I offered to examine him at his convenience. He told me that his schedule would not permit him time to see me on this trip to the Chicago area. I offered to be available to him and he accepted the offer.

Then as if I was the confessor and he the penitent I lowered the boom with a severe penance. "Fr. Ken," I told him, "if you want to keep your leg you must stop smoking now!" He looked at me with a determined face and put out his cigarette and said "So it will be." I will add here that I never knew him to smoke again.

Shortly afterwards, we departed company and he announced his plan to come up to Chicago at the end of his current tour for a physical.

That same weekend Kathy, Priscilla and I continued to go to the mission, Fr. Ken was gone before it was over. On the last night which was a Sunday we all were invited to the Chop House in Chicago to meet one last time. Because we had to travel in multiple cars we were asked by our hosts from California if we would drive some other people to the dinner. We stopped at The Rosemont Marriott and picked up three absolute strangers; an Irish tenor named Mark Forest, a Byzantine rite priest named Stephen Bahram and his male secretary. The six of us drove to the Chicago Chop House in an Audi A6 meant for only 5 passengers. Mark Forest was over six feet tall and Fr. Bahram was both tall and hefty. He looked and sounded like Jonathan Winters. His secretary was just as portly. We got to the restaurant on time and became quite well acquainted by the time we arrived due to the close quarters encountered during the ride.

In three days I met three people that would influence me and my family spiritually for years to come.

Chapter 15

Signs

"**A** sign without faith is merely a coincidence"
Father Ken Roberts

Several weeks passed and Fr. Ken called as promised to discuss his visit to Chicago. He announced that his secretary would not let him travel back to Chicago because he had to cancel part of his tour and it would hurt his reputation if it were discovered that he traveled elsewhere after the cancellation. I was at least puzzled by the logic but accepted it and offered to fly to his location to see him there and examine him regarding his leg complaints. He accepted my offer and I told him on a Monday that I would be there on Wednesday three days later. Having made the commitment I hung up the phone and turned to my wife and indicated that I just made a costly and impulsive decision in the name of gratitude. It would usually cost $800 or more for a short notice airplane reservation from Chicago to Dallas. I called American

Airlines and spoke with reservations. I waited for the bad economic news and was delighted to discover that I was eligible for the " 3 day advance" discount fare at the reduced price of $200. I booked the flight and packed my overnight bag and brought my medical bag along as well.

I was met at the airport by a nice southern lady with a deep southern drawl. She was chatty and gave me a tour on the way to the rectory where Ken was living at that time.

Ken met us at the door. He led me on an additional tour of the campus of the parish where he was assigned, introducing me to various people on the tour. He seemed to be a magnet with his charm and everyone liked him. That afternoon I examined him and discovered that in his right leg behind his knee he had a very loud bruit. A bruit is a sound that is made when blood rushes through an artery with a tight narrowing. I advised him that he needed to see a local vascular surgeon as soon as possible. I also discovered that he indeed had kept his promise to stop smoking.

As we spent the afternoon visiting Ken advised me that he was the recipient of frequent signs from the Virgin Mary. He said that he usually gets three red roses when he speaks in public about Mary or as an acknowledgement that his prayers have been heard. He took me to the garden and pointed to three red roses in full bloom among many other rose buds not yet opened. He told me that before my arrival this morning these roses were not yet opened.

I took that with a grain of salt at first, but remembering seeing him on the Oprah show when he demonstrated that he got his three red roses on live TV, I melted into belief.

The Oprah TV appearance by Fr. Roberts was marked by a discussion of Medjugorje and the appearance of the Blessed Virgin Mary. Fr. Ken said when he would give his talk that he always got three red roses when he spoke in public about

Mary. He pointed to Oprah's long sleeve dress and said "See I got my three red roses" and counted out three roses from Oprah's sleeves. Oprah said "That is not fair to say, I have four roses, two on each sleeve". Fr. Ken counted them aloud with Oprah watching. "Two roses on the right sleeve and one on the left." Oprah's response was "Oh my, I had four when I put this dress on, one must have fallen off" the audience applauded and Oprah seemed quite taken by the discovery.

After a pleasant afternoon and an evening out with more than generous host of Fr. Ken's friends, I retired to my hotel room with plans to leave after the weekday Mass that Fr. Ken would celebrate in the morning. I remember how amazed I was to see a full church for a weekday Mass. I left on the mid-morning plane for home considering the good deed I felt I had done and quite amazed at the charisma of this priest.

Months went by and we became close friends. He got his medical problem taken care of and was free of leg pain. My relationship with Ken started that way and has evolved into a very personal brother like friendship. I count him now as one of the family.

In September of that year my oldest daughter Natalie developed a severe case of homesickness after leaving for Holy Cross College two weeks earlier. Because of her tears Kathy and I considered flying her home for the weekend. When the cost of the short notice airplane ticket seemed about to break the budget I asked American Airlines for the three day short notice fair that I had used to visit Fr. Ken on my trip to Dallas. They told me point blank that there was no such fare and never had been. I asked them to look up my record kept for Advantage Miles and I was told that there was no record of me taking that trip. My immediate reaction was to share with Ken the amazing story of the cheap ticket that seemed to be a small miracle in light of the information I was given by American

Airlines. While I was on the phone with Fr. Ken I mentioned Natalie's sadness and homesickness. He said not to worry and he would pray about it. When I finished the conversation I called Natalie to give her the bad news about not being able to swing the expensive airfare. Her mood had changed to joy and she told me that she was happy now that she had been invited to a West Point ball, to be an escort for a cadet!

As I learned more about my new friend Ken I discovered that he had faith and was a great historian when it came to experiencing signs in his life. I witnessed several of these moments myself. The fact that he was a great preacher in his life and a good author as well leaves me feeling a bit inadequate in recounting some of his stories.

There was a time when he led a pilgrimage to Italy most of the people in the group had already heard about his unusual occurrence of receiving three red roses when he honored the Blessed Virgin Mary. It became the question of the day when they would all ask him if he had received his three red roses yet. They had multiple opportunities to witness these events during the tour of Italy. When they arrived at San Giovanni Rotundo and checked into the hotel, there in the lobby was a life sized statue of Padre Pio with a bunch of three roses in his hands. Fr. Ken had just finished leading the rosary on the bus and the last two glorious mysteries were about the Blessed Mother. The next morning he celebrated Holy Mass at the tomb of St. Padre Pio. At the Mass he again spoke about the Blessed Virgin Mary. Later that afternoon the group was taken on a tour of the monastery by one of the friars who took them to St. Padre Pio's cell. There on Padre Pio's bed were three fresh, red roses. Over the years of his ministry the three red roses continued to show up every time he preached about the Blessed Mother.

Another very interesting story I remember, Fr. Ken was on a speaking tour in Pennsylvania. He was on his way to Harrisburg, traveling with a prayer group in their bus through the state and they made several stops. None of the touring group was familiar with the area. It was about 4:45 PM and dinner was on everyone's mind. The driver stopped at a filling station and inquired about recommendations for eating establishments in the vicinity. They decided to go with the gas attendant's suggested Italian restaurant because it was supposed to be great Italian food and not too costly. About fifteen minutes' drive from where they were, the timing would be perfect for arrival at 5:00 PM dinner. On the way to the restaurant Father Ken led everyone in saying the glorious mysteries of the rosary and gave meditations on each one. The last two meditations were again on the subject of Mary. Upon entering the restaurant the proprietor handed Ken three red roses. The tour group gasped when they learned from the man that a lady had delivered them with instructions to give them to the priest who would be dining there that evening, at 5:00 PM, fifteen minutes before they knew the place existed. Along with the roses Ken was given a note that was intended for him as well. The note was written on a simple card. The message said "To my beloved son....from... Mary"

Yet another of the many examples and a difficult one to believe was the time Ken spoke at a Jesuit high school in a big eastern city. He had not originally intended to speak about Mary to this group, not the easiest topic to preach about at an all-male high school! Once he took the pulpit he changed his intended format and spoke about the rosary and the Blessed Mother. At the end of the talk, a senior came to the stage in front of the entire school and presented Father Roberts with three red roses. There were quite a few snickers from the all-male teenaged audience when the boy made his presentation.

What was even more extraordinary about this was that the boy's mother had asked him to bring them and give them to the speaker! The boy's mother knew about Fr. Ken and his often getting red roses, but nobody knew he was going to speak about Mary.

All these anecdotal stories are trimmings one could add as embellishments to the ministry of an itinerant missionary such as Ken. However my opinion about them being more than coincidences changed one weekend when Ken was visiting my home. My son Teddy was a sophomore in a local Catholic high school. He invited his entire baseball team to the house for a weekend afternoon bar-b-que and a swim party. Fr. Ken's charm and charisma drew the young men around him like the Pied Piper as he began telling stories. Ken changed the topic from a general discussion to one focused on the Church, the Holy Eucharist and in the end the Blessed Virgin Mary. He related his experiences of receiving three red roses to a very skeptical crowd of teenage boys. At the end of the long discussion the meal was ready and everyone sat down for dinner. No roses this time, chattered several of the boys. Suddenly the doorbell rang! A latecomer to the party stood at the door holding three red roses. Suddenly the chatter stopped and you could have heard a pin drop. Following this pause came a round of cheers! The boy with the roses explained that he stopped for flowers to give to his girlfriend on a date that evening and not wanting to leave them in the car where they might wilt he brought them into the house! After a brief explanation about the uproar he offered the roses to Fr. Ken. Ken advised the boy that having the roses present was a gift and that he should stick with his original intent to give the roses to his date. These young people were definitely given signs of God's love and truths that day. All of the young men left after dinner with a renewed sense of faith. Later we learned that the boy who brought the roses was seriously considering a vocation to the priesthood.

The Prophet Isaiah was given a sign, "Therefore the Lord Himself will give you this sign: The Virgin shall be with child, and bear a son, and shall name him Immanuel"(Isaiah 7:14). We know that this sign was confirmed with the birth of Jesus who was conceived in the womb of the Blessed Virgin Mary. He is Immanuel, meaning 'God with us". Fr. Ken tells of another incident in his life when he had an extraordinary experience regarding the Blessed Sacrament, which is God with us in the most Blessed sacrament of the Holy Eucharist. He was scheduled to be in Los Angeles to shoot film for his series on a EWTN Catholic Television Program. The television program was to be shot on the grounds of one of the seminaries in the Los Angeles area. The video crew drove over an hour to the studio in Burbank and when they arrived it was discovered that an important piece of equipment was missing and they were unable to make the recording without it. Facing a two hour delay before the taping could start; Fr. Ken decided to spend some time in the chapel making a Holy Hour in front of the Blessed Sacrament. He entered the chapel and knelt before the tabernacle. He was disturbed by an inner voice that said "I am not here." he looked up at the sanctuary light. It was burning brightly beside the tabernacle. He continued to pray and the same inner voice disturbed him again. Losing his peace, he left the chapel and went to find one of the seminary staff from whom he inquired if the Blessed Sacrament was in the tabernacle. He was told that it was removed for the summer break when the students left the campus. They had forgotten to extinguish the sanctuary lamp!

We are all accustomed to following signs in our travels. When making a long journey in unfamiliar areas we look for road signs. If our final destination is Chicago for example we will receive several signs that get us through other towns on our way even through detours until we reach our destination. These signs at detours are particularly important to us in finding our way back to the correct route home. If we did not believe that they were true signs of our destination we would not follow them. I am sure many people have shared the experience of misreading a sign and losing their way.

In our spiritual life our final destination is not a city named Chicago or any other place. Our spiritual destination is to be with God in heaven.

I got off track in my life in spite of a good foundation in faith. I took more than one detour and at times did not even know I was lost. Fortunately I was not hopelessly lost because of God's mercy and grace I found my way back to the road to salvation. His Grace came in the form of signs from good friends who helped light the way for me. When Ken came into my life I had found the right direction but was encountering problems that could lead to another detour. He was a very important signpost steering me away from any serious detour and on the right path to God's outstretched arms.

As I mentioned before Ken was also a light on the way for both of my daughters. Ken's sense of direction helped my daughter Priscilla when she approached him one day and inquired about a vocation as a nun. He turned to her and said "Forget it Priscilla, they don't make designer habits." I never saw her laugh so hard in my life. Several years later she quietly approached Fr. Ken in tears. She was in love but the man was not Catholic. Ken made arrangements to meet him and spent a great deal of time talking with him about the Catholic faith. The result was that Kirk decided to convert to Roman Catholicism and he and Priscilla announced their engagement. Priscilla married Kirk and they now have six beautiful children and she is now pregnant again. She attends daily Mass and the family prays together every day. They are a wonderful example of how a Catholic family should be. Andrew her first born is very intelligent and quick to learn. He has a very solid strength of character. He is deeply spiritual and sensitive to Godly things. Whenever Ken would visit me we would gather the family for prayers and a meal. On one occasion, Andrew who was only four years old at the time, surprised us all when he asked his mother in front of us all, if the other priest was coming back again today. Ken asked him, "what other priest?". "Fr. Pio" he answered innocently. "Who is Father Pio" we all asked; "Him", pointing to a statue of St. Padre Pio on the mantle in the kitchen. We were surprised at his answer and were amazed he would use the term "Fr. Pio" since we had never used that specific reference to St. Padre Pio in or out of the boy's presence. Sometime later, my father-in-law Walter entered the house and asked, "Who has been smoking Cigars?" Nobody had, it was a smoke free home. However it has been said that Padre Pio did and that the smell of cigar smoke was associated with his spiritual presence. Two years later the subject came up when Fr. Ken came to visit again. Ken asked him if he remembered the presence of Fr. Pio. Andrew responded affirmatively. His mother asked him what he remembered about it. He said the priest had said to him "Tell your mother I was here!"

During our many encounters with Fr. Ken he told us that everyone has a gift to share with other people. In addition to this he pointed out that no one has all the gifts but all must have the gift of faith, for without this gift any other gifts won't work as well as they could. He often preached "Never doubt the power of faith."

Ken has the gift of being charismatic. He admits he is very uncomfortable doing some things that priests are often called to do. The most onerous task for him is visiting the sick. This is a self-admitted personal weakness of his. My wife Kathy and I smile when we discuss this with him because that is our strength. I am a physician and Kathy is a nurse. Ken winces at the thought of a blood test let alone being at a hospital visiting the sick. He has however been called to this duty more than once in his priesthood. One of the priests in a rectory where he lived was a chaplain at a university hospital. He also had parish duties. Ken used to wonder what this priest's gift was because he was not gifted when he said Mass, gave terrible homilies, and always had the shortest line outside the confessional. He also had a reputation as being gruff. One day he went on a vacation and it became Ken's responsibility to fill in for him at the hospitals. As the regular chaplain he would spend hours a day at the hospital. Ken would rush from room to room say a quick prayer and bless the patient and be quickly on to the next one. One day a lady with tubes in every orifice and bedridden stopped him abruptly and asked, "When is the nice priest coming back, the one who sits and listens to you?" Ken said he learned a hard lesson in humility that day. The priest whom he had rashly judged had an extraordinary gift, the gift of the listening ear!

On a different occasion, Ken was vested for the 10 AM Mass when the pastor came and relieved him, asking him to answer a sick call of great urgency, at the local hospital. A young boy that Ken knew from the grade school where he did some teaching in the parish was near death. His parents had asked for Ken. Keep in mind that this was not Ken's gift. He was petrified as he relates it and I found that plausible, knowing Ken's aversion to these matters. When he got to the hospital room both parents were at the boy's bedside weeping. The boy was ghastly white in appearance and soaked in sweat. His fever was very high. The doctors had told the parents there was little hope. Fr. Ken took out his bible and read the story of the centurion who came to Jesus for a healing for his servant. The centurion was a pagan Roman yet he had the faith that Jesus could heal him. Jesus said he had not found such faith in all of Israel. The Centurion had told Jesus just say the word and his servant would be healed. He believed. He had the gift of real faith when Jesus told him his servant will live. At every mass we say the words of the Centurion just before Holy Communion. "Lord I am not worthy that you should enter under my roof, but only say the word and my soul will be healed."

Ken turned to the parents after he had read the passage from scripture and after anointing the child. He asked them if they really believed that scripture. The boy's mother was a Roman Catholic married to a Baptist superintendent of the areas Baptist Bible schools. So, Ken challenged them to really believe with the faith of the Centurion and their son would live! He blessed them both and left quickly to get back for noon Mass. Leaving the patients room he was met by a doctor who said you had better pray the Lord takes that boy, if he survives this fever he will have terrible brain damage. He has no chance of living a normal life! Ken recalled feeling so guilty at this point, challenging the faith of the doomed boy's parents that way. He vested for noon Mass and after the Gospel he told the worshipers what he had done. He said I am now going to challenge this congregation. If there is just one person at this Mass with the faith of the Centurion then that boy will recover and live a normal life. If there is not one person here with that kind of faith then God help this parish. He did not give a homily, instead led the congregation in the Apostle's Creed. I believe in God.....He checked his watch. !t was 12:35.

After Mass was over he returned to the rectory for lunch and the house keeper informed him that the hospital had called before the end of Mass. The boy had recovered at 12:35! He was awake and eating his first meal in days.

When the Centurion arrived home his servants met him and told him of the miraculous recovery. It was the exact hour that Jesus said he would live. Somebody, perhaps more, in that parish had the faith of the Centurion.

In Ken's retirement he has been called again to the humility that befits a true servant of God. He is the cook and dishwasher for the small community in which he lives. He has devoted hours at the side of two devoted friends who are very ill. At the time of the writing of this book he attended one of these friends at the bedside during the hours of her death. I am sure he is one of God's special apostles.

Chapter 16
God is Faithful to His People

My relationship with Fr. Stephen Barham began the night after I met Fr. Roberts for the first time. As I mentioned in a previous chapter we met coincidentally as I was drafted to be one of the drivers to a Sunday night dinner at the Chop House in Chicago. I sat with Stephen Barham at the table while we all ate a steak dinner and enjoyed some excellent red wine thanks to our generous host from California. Steve was a portly and jolly man with a booming voice and a laugh to match. He defined the word gregarious. His Roman collar tightly fit around his thick neck was accented by a heavy gold chain and a gold cross that was his trademark. He introduced himself to all of us by relating the history of who he was and how he became an archimandrite in the Byzantine rite of the Roman Catholic Church. At the same conference in Chicago where we first met Fr. Steve we also met the famous Irish tenor, Mark Forest. Due to our long, engaged conversation time passed without us realizing how late it was. They both had to catch a plane for their next engagement but it seemed unlikely that we would make the airport in time to catch it. Steve told me not to worry and just to drive to O'Hare airport. He assured me that he would pray for the intercession of St Raphael, the Archangel, since he even got upgrades to first class when he prayed to this archangel, and the Archangel Raphael never let him down. The trip to the airport only took 25 minutes instead of the usual hour. I was able to stay in the center lane as everyone got out of my way. I never had a trip to Chicago's O'Hare airport that easy or that fast before or since. We made it with time to spare. If you ever need a strong advocate to intercede for you, try St. Raphael.

Stephen came from a family of preachers in the Assembly of God Church. He grew up in ministry to Christian people. Even before he became an ordained Assembly of God minister he had accumulated a long list of certified healings by praying over the ill and infirm. Steven devoted himself to the advanced study of theology in quest of his second PhD, and he told me that one day he realized then that he was in the wrong Church. He knew from the study of scripture and Christian tradition that the true Church started with Peter and that there was a line of ordained priests that went back to him. He studied carefully and determined that he wanted to be a Greek Orthodox priest. At the time he saw no difference between that and Roman Catholicism. He chose it because he had a worldly appetite for the fancy gold trappings of chains and crosses, traditional garments and the splendor of the architecture and design of the Greek Orthodox churches. He also had a passion for Icons of the type that the Greeks did so well. His worldly passion for those trappings and his appetite for good food and drink were equally balanced. They were only surpassed by his intellectual curiosity and burning love for the Truth and Jesus' Church. The fact that the Greeks did not require celibacy and he was engaged to be married also came to bear on his ultimate decision. Stephen filled the room with his presence in social discourse and humor. He filled Cathedrals with his Assembly of God skills at preaching from the pulpit. Stephen was a living contrast between the zest for Spiritual life and the zest for the gifts of human life. He was a very portly man tipping the scales over three hundred pounds and wearing colorful sashes around his huge belly over the deliberately ornate buttons on his Archimandrite cassock. The heavy gold cross hung from his neck and rested on an angle on the top of his corpulent abdomen. He would often say in humor that the body is supposed to be the Temple of the Holy Spirit, and hugging his hips and waist he would suggest, look at me I am building a Basilica!

Stephen spent 16 1/2 years as a Greek Orthodox priest when again, he came to the realization that he was still in the wrong Church, He sought counsel from his bishop on the process to become a traditional Catholic priest with allegiance to the Pope. His bishop helped him make arrangements to concelebrate Mass with the Bishop of the Washington D.C. Diocese at the National Cathedral. This process publicly acknowledged that he was in allegiance to the Pope. Stephen chose deliberately to join the Byzantine rite because of familiarity with the Eastern Church traditions and garb and the title Archimandrite. It was during the later half of his priesthood that I was fortunate enough to find myself dining for the first time with this most extraordinary and cherished friend.

Fr. Stephen had his share of ill health. When he was an Assembly of God minister his doctor diagnosed colon cancer in its later stages. With metastases to his liver he had six months to live. He continued his ministry in spite of his health and on a subsequent consultation with his doctor discovered that the cancer had disappeared. His Church, community, and the medical doctors all considered this miraculous. He took Meridian for his obesity and developed a nagging heart condition because of damage to his aortic valve (the main valve that lets blood out of the heart to the rest of the body). In fact, much later after joining a class action suit he was awarded 1 million dollars posthumously. During his ministry subsequent to the colon cancer he developed kidney cancer and had a kidney removed without sequelae, he continued on in his ministry working tirelessly.

A great preacher and story teller, he told the audience how he originally came from a strong Pentecostal family with several members all ordained ministers. He recounted how he met Rev Jimmy Swaggart in a Baton Rouge, Louisiana restaurant and walked up to him to introduce himself. Fr. Stephen was dressed in black clericals as he did so. Jimmy Swaggart was well known for his serious anti-Catholicism and was a little disturbed to meet this character in a black clerical suit and roman collar. Fr. Barham smiled as he told him I used to be an Assembly of God minister like you and 23 members of my family are also very much involved with the Assembly of God ministries, one of them is the district moderator of the Assembly of God for this area. Swaggart was very confused, "Then how come we are both going in the opposite direction?" "I don't know about you but I am going to heaven", was Fr. Steve's quick answer. This was followed by the big body shaking laugh with matching grin from ear to ear. Yes, he could definitely have doubled for Jonathan Winters, in looks and in humor. Fr. Steve also had a very serious side. He still retained a strong and powerful evangelical style of preaching which held the attention of the audience and evoked their response with much laughter to his tent like evangelical gatherings but now in giant sized arenas.

When I first became seriously ill in 1996 he was one of the rocks of solace upon whom I depended for support. His sense of my heart ailment then was that I had no immediate concerns about mortality. I knew then he seemed to have a sixth sense about these things and felt quite reassured. When Fr. Stephen developed a new cancer in his remaining kidney I was there to support him. He had one half of his remaining kidney removed and the result was not good. Although cured of cancer again he was consigned to dialysis for renal failure unless he was able to have a transplant. Because of his worldwide missions he did not want to have hemodialysis and chose peritoneal dialysis. That is a procedure done by the patient at night during the usual eight hours of sleep. A special permanent catheter is placed thru the abdominal wall into the peritoneal space and at night large quantities of fluids are infused into the peritoneum and after a wait the fluids are then drained out. This can be done with portable equipment that automatically performs this task but it is bulky and requires the use of large quantities of dialysis fluid that is fresh daily. He continued his worldwide ministry with this handicap and never missed an appointed time to minister to people or to preach. In his travels all over the world his dialysis equipment and fluids were always shipped ahead of him and they never went missing.

He was tough, and at times he would preach with fluid overload to the point of breathlessness due to his renal failure and his failing heart caused by the faulty heart valve. One day he confided in me that he was frustrated that he could not do more than he was doing due to these problems. I spoke candidly to him about kidney transplant. He remarked that he had gotten an opinion and was told there were two waiting lists. One for five years to make sure the cancer was cured and the other for five years to actually get a kidney. I intervened through a kidney specialist that I knew and we found a transplant surgeon who was willing to list him on both lists simultaneously.

After he was listed, I felt I had let him down, because he still had a long frustrating wait. He reassured me that I should never make God laugh by telling God my plans. I should leave this to the Lord. He was certainly suffering, but I relaxed and accepted his advice. He then told me for the second time his favorite little parable about himself. He said, "You see, whenever I have to travel I get upgraded to first class! If I find myself in coach I just pray for assistance from St. Raphael the Archangel. Invariably I get the call to move up before the plane leaves." So I am not worried if it is not apparent now, but this wait will be shorter if it is God's will'. Less than a year after that discussion Fr. Stephen called me to tell me he was getting on a flight from Dallas to Chicago. His pager had gone off and his destination was RUSH University hospital for a new kidney!

As joyful as this event was it did have a bit of a price. Stephen developed a wound dehiscence post operatively from a MRSA infection. This means his wound opened up to the outer lining of the peritoneum and had to be packed daily until it closed. This however was not justification to continue hospitalization. He was not allowed to leave town because of the continuous need for medical supervision of his wound his infection and his anti-rejection medication. He checked into a residential hotel in Chicago, the Presidential Towers where he had daily visits from a nurse wound specialist. And on weekends was able to retreat to the suburbs to stay with our family. I had the needed skills to change his dressing and substitute for the visiting nurse.

It was about this time that Fr Barham became entwined with the love life of my oldest daughter Natalie. She had met a very important young man who eventually became her husband. Fr. Steve had prayed for the relationship to crystallize and it did. He met the young man for lunch in the city one day and was instrumental in getting him to come back to the Catholic faith. Young Steve developed a strong bond with Father Stephen.

As Fr. Stephen became independent of the need for daily dressing changes he resumed his ministry. Several years passed and his heart disease slowly got worse. I spoke to him about it many times but he took it his stride and made a personal decision not to pursue valve repair. In the summer of 1999 my middle daughter got engaged to Kirk and they decided to ask Fr. Barham to officiate at their wedding. He happily agreed and changed his missionary calendar to accommodate their January 6, 2000 date. Everything was set but the weather, which he advised us to leave in God's hands.

Tragedy Struck! Less than two weeks before the wedding Mark Forest, the third important person from that fateful weekend at the Rosemont in Chicago, called with the sad news that Fr. Stephen had died suddenly of heart failure in his doctor's waiting room. The cold dark days of December surrounded us in our grief. I dropped everything to represent the family in Dallas at Fr. Stephen's funeral.

I was met at the airport by a driver who was assisting the parish. He was a good young man and his services were volunteered to the parish for these types of occasions. He drove me to Fr. Stephen's father's home where I paid my respects and met other members of Stephen Barham's inner circle. They all made sure I was well taken care of and Mark Forest was also there. The two of us agreed to share a room at a local hotel.

The next morning I arrived at the church for the funeral which was one of the largest churches I have ever seen and it had standing room only. Many of Stephen Barham's friends, family and many Catholic Church dignitaries were there. The eulogy was given by Fr. Stephens's former Greek Orthodox bishop. He spoke at length and eloquently about this special servant of God whose ordained priesthood from his Greek Orthodox ordination until his death as a Catholic Byzantine rite Archimandrite priest was exactly 33 years. A point used by the bishop to associate Stephen's priest hood closely with the life of Christ.

After the funeral ended my driver who was waiting for me in the back of the church took me back to the airport. During the half hour ride we spoke. He asked me," Who was that priest and why was the crowd so large?" I responded the best way I could still choked up from the grief of the experience. I told him that Fr. Barham was a joyous servant of the Lord whose constant message to all that would listen was, "Our Lord is a faithful God and is fiercely loyal to his people." At that very moment a large black Mercedes drove by in the passing lane at extreme speed. The driver was a blonde woman, but the license plate said one word. "God"!

Chapter 17

Friends in the Lord

Shortly after my return from Medjugorje I got my second phone call from Andy Zovko. He was not simply inquiring regarding the accommodations he had arranged. He was most interested in the spiritual effects of my pilgrimage. Andy was a very devout Catholic and a very holy man. With this phone call we started a 20 year relationship that had a great influence on the further evolution of my spiritual rebirth. Throughout the time I knew Andy I would only see him a few times at healing services which he conducted with the permission of the Chicago Archdiocese. Most of our friendship was conducted over the phone due to his busy schedule and my busy schedule. He was a constant in my life and I am grateful for that. He introduced me to Fr. Charles Becker who is currently my spiritual advisor and confessor. Fr. Charlie and Andy led many pilgrimages to Medjugorje since I was there. He asked me many times if I wanted to go back and I never felt the need to make that trip again. I did send my daughter Natalie when she was in high school with a group led by Fr. Ken Roberts. I learned about Fr. Roberts from Andy Zovko. Andy once told me that all of his friends were friends in The Lord. I discovered as time went on that this was a requirement for me as well. My new born again faith demanded it.

It was not that everyone I considered to be a friend had to be saintly, I knew better than that. All my friends have a goodness about them that at least makes them open to the healing Grace of God. Not all are committed believers. Most are and the rest I pray for regularly. I have learned to recognize those who are not open to God's grace. I don't befriend them, but I do pray for them.

Father Charles Becker is my spiritual advisor and confessor. I was introduced to him by Andy Zovko. Father also had a conversion to stronger faith after going to Medjugorje. He began to more openly demonstrate his priesthood and became a public witness to his faith by being sure to wear his roman collar, instead of the casual dress of priests in our time. He made his life a symbol of The Roman Catholic Church. His courage, strength, and character in this are signs of his love for God. If you ever meet him he would be glad to tell you himself how we are all not perfect and need that inner strength and God's grace to avoid sin and keep God's commandments. I know he prays for me as I do for him and for his ministry. His presence at my side during critical illness left me with a real sense of hope and God's love.

It was less than a year after my trip to Medjugorje that I went to a mission devoted to the Blessed Virgin Mary at Notre Dame University in South Bend Indiana. It was a three day event. The first evening it was raining and a procession of all the attendee's was scheduled by candlelight to the famous Notre Dame Grotto. I was with Kathy and we were in the midst of a large crowd of people when I thought I spotted Fr. Phil Pavich standing on the side of the path. As I was pointing him out to Kathy he looked at me and grinned and said "Hello doctor it's nice to see you again, I am glad you are here."

Kathy turned to me and said "That must have been one memorable confession." This was the first time I had actually been able to talk to Phil Pavich since I went to him for the Sacrament of Penance in Medjugorje! His capacity for recall amazed me then. Since then he has become a family friend and we have enjoyed his friendship and his company several times. He currently lives in Chicago.

It was shortly after that trip to Notre Dame that Kathy and I decided to join a prayer group that met on Wed. evenings at St. Mary Parish in Buffalo Grove, Illinois. I won't mention all of those people by name, but they are all now close friends in the Lord. The Pastor of St Mary Church, Marc Reszel, is also a friend in the Lord. He came to St. Mary when my family had started to grow and spread out to other parishes. He helped keep us together at least on Sundays for Holy Mass by opening up lines of communication outside of the geographical limits of his parish. He often comes to dinner at our home where he has spirited debates with both my daughters, who look forward to his presence at dinner parties. He traveled with us to Rome and performed the wedding ceremony for my oldest daughter Natalie and her husband Steve. In June of 2008 when I was critically ill he came to the hospital urgently to anoint me with the Sacrament of the Sick.

Standing out from this above mentioned group is Pat Dorian. She was in the convent preparing for final vows when she changed her plans for vocation as a nun to wife and mother. Pat was a dynamo, and still is. One could say that she was a "community organizer for spiritual need". She and her husband Tom are close friends in the Lord. They are retired now and winter in the Naples, Florida area and summer in Wisconsin. We still communicate regularly and Pat freely shares her religious zeal with us and others.

Mark Forest is a well-known Irish tenor. He lives just outside of Washington DC and has performed for several presidents. He has a golden voice and has devoted his life and talents to Catholic and Christian ideals. His tours are usually by bus and he gives concerts in churches and church auditoriums. His talents would command a worldwide celebrity class if he wanted to choose a secular path. I have been fortunate to know him for many years. We met at a Marion Mission in Chicago at the same time I met two other important and complex people to whom I have devoted two previous chapters.

Mark has been the soloist at my daughter Priscilla's wedding and my son Ted's wedding. I have had the pleasure of having him in my home for private concerts on two occasions with many friends in attendance. He gives a strong Catholic example in his personal life as well. He has three sons with metabolic disease that attacks the central nervous system. To them and the rest of his children, both he and Muriel his wife are committed and loving parents.

We were in a bar together sharing a bottle of wine one night when he was on tour, passing through Chicago. The news came on over the television that Princess Diana had died. He had a brief moment of sadness on his face which I have never seen before or since. Considering the difficult life he has and his openness to God's plan he is otherwise always happy and smiling, and had been a beacon of hope and support for me and many other people who have endured difficult trials in life.

During the difficult days of college life struggling to compete for a place in medical school I became fast friends with a man of great character and perseverance. We endured the difficult race together and I was accepted to medical school and Bob was not. I knew how painful that was as he was so deserving of a seat in medical school based on his performance in college. Bob ultimately became a medical doctor and specialized in neonatology. We are still friends today, not so much because of the bond we made competing in college, but because of his great devotion to the Lord which he proclaims by the way he lives his life. We are both prayer partners at times storming Heaven with our prayers for one another in times of crisis. Whenever I remember Bob Manniello it brings to mind the Gospel of John, Chapter 13, verse 35; "This is how all will know that you are My disciples, if you have love for one another".

David Stein is a devout Jew. He follows the Lord in the tradition of the Old Testament. He has been a close personal friend and a guiding light thru the most troubling times I have experienced. If I find myself in a difficult spot I usually find David there holding out his hand to help me. In spite of our different perspectives on salvation I know he is one of the Lord's special servants and his friendship one of God's gifts to me.

David and Carol Mc Avoy are my neighbors for the past 27 years in Dennis Ma. They have spent countless hours on their knees for me and my family during troubled times. We have returned the favor. Although we see them only when enjoying our summer home we are bonded through our love and trust in the Lord.

There is a very unique friar of the Franciscan order who wishes anonymity in this writing. He has been a special spiritual guide in my life starting the first year after I developed a life altering and life threatening illness. I will respect his privacy but will allude to the crucial role he has played in the most recent part of my life as I write the final part of this book you will learn about his participation in this respect.

Steve Arcenaux my Cajun friend from New Orleans was the one who said the "Grace before Meals" in Medjugorje. He and I have stayed close friends after all these years. Steve introduced me to the joys of deer hunting in Mississippi and to the special restaurants known only to residents of New Orleans specializing in Cajun cuisine. It was Steve's prayer group that made me one of them on my trip to Medjugorje.

I cannot conclude this Chapter without mentioning Benn Gilmore. He is my best friend. We met in San Diego when we first started in the Navy during the Vietnam War. We bonded immediately and have been friends for life. Benn is currently retired from medicine and deeply involved with a Nondenominational Christian Church. He goes all over the world and builds churches and schools. He has even delivered sermons. Benn and I have a relationship based on endless conversations and shared thoughts that are based around the content of St. Paul's Letter to the Philippians, chapter 4, verse 8, " Finally, brothers, whatever is true, whatever is honorable, whatever is just, whatever is pure, whatever is lovely, whatever is gracious, if there is any excellence and if there is anything worthy of praise, think about these things."

Part 3

Walking up Calvary with Jesus and the Holy Spirit

Chapter 18

Coming to Terms with Mortality

L ying in bed in the critical care unit in June of 2008, I was immersed in the trappings of technology. Intravenous fluids flow into my veins and parades of doctors coming and going, I hear the irregular ticking of my heart amplified by the monitor and see the chaotic rhythm on a flat screen in living color. My mind drifts back to the beginning when I first came to terms with my own mortality.

The month was May, 12 years earlier, the day Sunday, when I first felt the irregular flutter in my chest and ignored it. The following morning the beginning of my long work week I found myself suddenly slumping into the arms of Marlette who had followed me down the hallway asking for a signature as I raced to start my day. Unable to hold me up she eased me to the floor and called for help. The staff nurses from the nursing home ran down the hall behind a wheelchair. I recovered, refused the ride and walked back to the nurse's office under their watchful eye. No chest pain, no shortness of breath, no sweating and the lightheadedness had cleared. I pronounced myself healthy and stable. Wisely they would not accept my own self-diagnosis. We compromised. I called my friend David Stein a cardiologist. He told me to call 911 for a ride to the emergency room. I intended on driving myself when a nurse said no. Several, insisted that at least one of them drive me to the hospital.

Dr. Stein was already in the ER when I walked in, shortly after so was my wife Kathy and my partner Sandra Garretson. The staff danced attendance upon me as if I were a visiting dignitary. First there was an electrocardiogram, then blood tests and an IV. The technician from the cardiology department rolled an echocardiograph machine up to my gurney and proceeded to search my chest for echoes of my cardiac anatomy. Dave Stein looked at the graph for a long time. He turned to me and advised me that I had a dilated heart with congestive heart failure. Continuing to speak while that news was settling in he outlined he plan for me to go to Loyola University hospital immediately. I balked! Without hesitation he turned to my wife and asked "Helicopter or ambulance?" As the seriousness of this began to flood my senses and anxiety rose I was loaded into an ambulance for the 45 minute drive with sirens blowing.

Reassurance came in the person of Dr. Marc Silver at Loyola. He had a serious demeanor about him and a staff to match. I learned he was the chief of the Heart Failure Institute and Heart transplant program at the University. After three days and a left heart catheterization with angiogram and a right heart biopsy he painted a picture for me that I might live with! The prescriptions and the salt free diet and the loss of martini privileges seemed a small price to pay to avoid the dreaded outcome of end stage heart failure and heart transplant. We had an uneasy pact. He would guide me through the illness; I could keep my present heart. The unanswered question for us both was; for how long?

Life for a person with chronic congestive heart failure changes in many ways. I mentioned the anxiety that came with the knowledge of the diagnosis. Stamina wanes and fatigue becomes a part of life. Shortness of breath limits physical activity and the confidence that comes with manhood fades away into the fear that I can no longer protect myself or my loved ones with physical effort. My wife started looking for a condominium so that I would not be challenged with stairs. During the first year I prayed not to be in the 1/3 of cases that are known to get worse fast. That was what happened to my brother and he died in the third month of the disease. Carrying that with me wore me down and I never found peace on my own. The peace came from reassurances given by the spiritual people in my life. Fr. Charles Becker came to Loyola and gave me a brown scapula which I have saved and worn constantly. It gave me spiritual strength and Fr. Becker's friendship. He became my spiritual advisor and confessor from that time on in my life. When I returned home and resumed practicing medicine I knew better how it feels to be on the other end of the stethoscope. My wife changed too. She became my perpetual guardian always looking over my shoulder and watching over me like a living guardian angel. The first year was bad and the course was downhill. Clearly it seemed that I was in early trouble with my heart failure when I stopped being able to do stairs or climb ramps without profound breathlessness.

In those days we had many friends who prayed hard for my recovery and during travels to my summer home in Dennis, Ma., we would stop to see the Friars of the Primitive Order and bring them groceries on our way to the airport. It happened, one visit that I was doing quite poorly and I met for the first time my close friend, a friar from that group who took an interest in my personal and spiritual health. He put his hand on my shoulder the day we met and simply said come with me pointing at a flight of stairs to climb. I indicated that I did not think I could make it up the stairs in my condition. He turned and asked "Are you in a state of grace?" I nodded yes and he said "then God's angels will see to it that you have help". Climbing those stairs turned out to be unexpectedly easy for me. Once upstairs we knelt in the chapel and the friar took out the Blessed Sacrament from the tabernacle and we prayed together for a long time. The content and words of those prayers I have kept private at his request. When I left him I knew that I must spend an hour in front of the Blessed Sacrament every day for a year.

Weeks later I met Dr. Silver at Loyola and he started me on a breakthrough drug for heart failure. That drug and the prayers with the Blessed Sacrament I believe were instrumental in my early recovery and stability for the next 8 years. But finally the drugs stopped working. The prayers made me more holy and I began to ready myself for death. I continued to press hard at living, but every day became more challenging than the day before. I practiced hiding the symptoms and fooled some friends but not my wife or family and certainly not my partner or the nurses that I worked with every day. If someone saw me hesitate when walking down a hall and rest, or doing the same walking from my car into the hospital or office, I would explain that I had sciatica and it was slowing me down. I lied about the breathlessness, the weakness, and the light headedness. In the months leading up to my final hospitalization my oxygen levels dropped so low with my blood pressure that I even had multiple episodes of public urinary incontinence which added the additional burden of embarrassment to that which I was already carrying.

Now I was back in the hospital because of several black-outs which caused me to fall to the floor and dramatic weight gain in spite of eating very little for months. My legs were like logs filled with fluid. My lungs were stiff from fluid overload. My oxygen was dangerously low in the high 70's to low 80'(93 plus on room air is normal). My blood pressure was 75/40. My neck veins were budging and my face was blue-gray. I was in the office trying to work when I collapsed and had to go to the local hospital 911.

I woke up to the pain in my chest from an elective cardio version. It felt like I was kicked. I was told it wouldn't hurt! The procedure worked but there was no improvement in my symptoms when the atrial fibrillation was shocked into normal sinus rhythm. When the light anesthetic wore off my medical team was assembled around the bed. The news had finally come. Nothing would save me except a heart transplant. While waiting for arrangements to be finalized I learned that my "Friend in the Lord" Andy Zovko had passed on to his eternal reward. I wondered if I might be joining him soon. Kathy knowing this possibility never left my side day or night.

Transferred down to Christ Hospital in Oak Lawn, Illinois Dr. Silver made the same declaration. The testing began for determining my status. Now I realized the inevitable had come. I knew my future and it was more than I thought I could handle. Anxiety overwhelmed me. I thought of Jesus in the Garden of Gethsemane sweating blood because He knew what He must endure. I prayed all the time. A special prayer taught me by Fr. John Sweeny of the Friars of the Primitive Order rolled off my lips over and over again." Most Sacred Heart of Jesus make my heart beat like Yours". I grew weaker rapidly. Unlike Jesus in the Garden I was not left alone to deal with my future. Kathy, my sister Kate, my children and grandchildren, many good friends came and counted time with me. The poet and novelist Delmore Schwartz once wrote, "Time is the fire in which we burn" for me the remaining time which was all I saw ahead of me, was that fire. The urgency accelerating, my kidneys were not cooperating. My creatinine levels were too high for cyclosporine, an essential anti-rejection drug. If they were to use that drug with my creatinine over 2.0 I would need dialysis. It was difficult for me to accept that the hope of transplant might be off the table. They talked of left ventricular assist devices as a bridge to transplant and now they were without hope that I could have that bridge. An alternate path called destination therapy was offered that might keep me alive. I hoped aloud that this would allow my kidneys to return to normal function. Their response gave no reassurance of this to me. The day they demonstrated the devices to me and to Kathy we had a frank discussion about which one I did not want. Benn Gilmore showed up at my bedside shortly after that. We held hands and prayed the "Our Father" together. Then with Benn and Kathy as my witnesses I left the decision to the Lord.

Days in intensive care turned into weeks. There was still no decision about which LVAD device to install. There was a glimmer of hope, in that with the 6 intravenous drugs I now depended on for life itself, my kidney function improved to 1.4. The bad news was there was no way to stop the drugs now and my lungs were filling with fluid. Every breath was a struggle. There was pain everywhere. Each blood draw required multiple attempts. The highest count I recall was nine. My chest hurt from each breath. My back raged at me with each turn in bed. The bladder catheter was both an instrument of torture as well as one of the chains I wore to keep me in bed. Bondage is the cruelest of all torments! The nurses and the doctors focused on measurements of my cardiac output to control the drugs. The right heart pressures were measured twice a shift until one evening the catheter in my pulmonary artery moved and the pressures could not be measured. The team decided to replace the entire catheter with a new one. Other tubes were placed. I felt a sense of detachment and fear as I watched, heard, and felt them work. They took my left wrist and cut open a hole in the skin to introduce an arterial line for measuring blood pressure. My pressure now was so low that a cuff wouldn't measure it. Hours went by and the team decided to take me down to fluoroscopy to better guide the replacement of the critical right heart catheter. There while lying flat on the table I became hopelessly breathless and lost all consciousness.

"Out of the depths I cry to you o Lord.
Lord hear my voice!
Let your ears be attentive to the voice of my supplications!"

Psalm 129 1-2

As this was happening I remember the pain of breathing and the lights in the procedure room. These were followed by nothingness at first and then a return to awareness. Now I was in a gray place there was no up or down; nothing to see, nothing to feel, just gray. In an instant I felt a ripping throughout my entire body. Searing pain was everywhere like a tearing sensation. The thought came to me that was the ripping away of my soul from my body. Immediately following this never to be forgotten sensation was a voice, an ancient, accusatory, relentless voice. The voice was reporting my sinful life to me and simultaneously revealing to me in life sized images that would change with each accusation the nature of each and every sin I had ever committed. I learned of the effects of those sins. Each one was like a pebble dropped in a pond its effect spreading out from the source like waves onto others. The sins of omission were detailed as well. Taking the Lord's name in vain and not prayer injured the Lord and caused Him much pain. I learned he sought no vengeance even though He felt the pain but, He was infinitely just.

I was afraid. The voice continued. The parade of sins over time continued. I was outside of time and the eternity of this parade cannot be described from the vantage point where I viewed it and experienced each offense. I logically reasoned that I was standing before the judgment seat of God. The voice I heard was that of Satan. I felt weakness, sadness, shame, but mostly horror and a need to give up and accept hopelessness. Logic told me that I was saved; I had received the Last Sacraments and absolution from a priest recently. I had even obtained a plenary indulgence. Yet here I was, pressure mounting to despair listening to Satan describe to God how unworthy I was to be saved.

I began to pray directly to God the Father. I addressed him by all the names I knew him by. Abba, Yahweh, and Father: I got no response. I saw nothing, heard nothing, felt nothing. Despair crowded me and reached for me and I fought it off. "Jesus" I prayed, perhaps screamed, "Save me, Jesus mercy, Jesus I know you are my Savior." Nothing happened, no response, no message, no sensation, no light, just the overwhelming, choking of despair. The grayness grew. I called out "Spirit save me!!!!!!!!"

It was not a voice. It was not a vision. It was a sensation with a message. The Spirit responded and the message was "Call upon Mary"! I was interrupted by the voice. "Now you will spend eternity with me" when you pray to Her you will blaspheme and be damned. I hesitated, recalling the theological controversy about praying to Mary vs. asking Mary to intercede. Then The Spirit commanded me again "Call Mary." I chose my words carefully and suddenly there was light and the face of a beautiful woman, she was crowned and clothed in blue, white and gray, her eyes were dark, blue I remember. She stared at me and I at her. She raised her left hand and placed it on my face. I felt the softness of her touch. Her fingers were spread so my eyes could see. She addressed me by name. "It's ok Ted, go back everything will be alright"!

Chapter 19
While I Was Away

When I was brought back from the fluoroscopy lab I was blue black in color and lifeless. Emergency measures taken advanced quickly to the ultimate attempt at rescue. My lifeless body rolled into the operating room for placement on the heart-lung machine and then the installation of a Left Ventricular Assist Device (artificial heart).

Those who witnessed this can relate the events only through their tears, so my story is a fusion of their memories. My friends and family were suffering then. I was not conscious.

My sister Kate, recalled from boarding her plane, returned to my side. My wife was dysfunctional by various accounts, related by my children, curled up in a lounge chair, crying wrapped in a white blanket in the fetal position. Natalie came and collapsed in tears. My good friend Jim Forsythe came and collapsed in grief at the door to my room. Tony called and was on his way when Kathy managed to tell him it was futile and to go home instead and pray. Priscilla had the faith of the centurion and knelt by my bed and led others in prayer. Bill my brother-in-law who is tougher than nails wept at my bedside then threatened me with a dire forecast that if I did not wake up, O'Bama would win. My Franciscan Friar upon whom I so deeply depended drove all night from the east coast to my side. My son, Teddy drove in from Minneapolis leaving Maureen to fend for herself with a newborn baby named Grace. Dave and Jill Stein came and helped give advice to Kathy. Benn Gilmore came and did for my Kathy what I would have done for his Kathy. He sized up the situation and warned of the unlikely occurrence that I would not survive and leveled with my dear wife and family and my Franciscan Friar.

The surgeon pressed Kathy for permission to place the LVAD. He indicated to her which one was the only one he had time to install. She remembered my discussion with her and refused consent as this was the one device I told her I would not ever want. She was my medical POA and next of kin. The choice was hers only. The pressure was on. She was also burning in the fire of time. After consulting with my Franciscan Friar she consented and the rescue proceeded. When they wheeled me back to the ICU they assigned three nurses to watch me constantly. I have never known this type of intensive care in my entire medical career. I was astounded to learn of it. As I lay there the explanations were given for what they had done. I was now dependent on a machine for each pulse of blood through my body. My kidneys had failed and my liver was shocked. I was canary yellow from the liver injury. The words spoken were painful for all to hear. In five days they would know if my brain was destroyed. If so they could turn me off. I was elsewhere; not aware; in no real physical pain. Time burned for all!

Chapter 20

Another Cross to Carry

I remember Alex' face and the way he gripped my hand. He was asking me over and over again to blink, to squeeze his hand. I did, he grinned from ear to ear. He dropped my hand. It fell heavily to the bed as he hurried out of the room. I tried to lift my own hand and it was too heavy and would not move. I slept again. Again, there appeared Alex, following the same routine this time holding out a pen for me to write. My hand was too heavy, I tried and tried and again, I slept. Awake again, I felt a searing pain in my throat and realized why Alex wanted me to write. I could not talk around the breathing tube in my trachea. Alex pulled at my hand again offered me a pen again and I scribbled on the page some sign of consciousness and a functioning brain. The exercise seemed endless and repeated itself over and over. I slept less and felt more. Not only were my arms heavy, but the rest of me would not move on command. The nurses had to move me for days and then one day the doctor managing my ventilator promised on rounds in the morning, the tube in my wind pipe would be extracted by noon. I managed to find the clock; only six hours to go!

The team came in pulled the tube, I coughed a hoarse cough and felt the pain in my chest and that in my side. I heard the pump rhythmically banging in the background. Before I could ask, someone explained that I had been attached to "Big Bertha", the refrigerator sized heart pump that was sending my own blood coursing through my arteries. When my arms and hands would move I explored my connection to the machine, unable yet to lift my head I could only feel the hoses affixed to my left side. The wound hurt. I could imagine what it might be like to be stabbed. The nurse, usually Alex, dressed the wound daily.

When I realized the hoses were connected to an external device similar to that which I rejected, I was only relieved to be alive. Discovering how my wife had struggled with the decision to place this peripheral LVAD I reassured her that my gratitude exceeded my premorbid ignorance. In fact, I marveled at the way I felt on the once prohibited machine.

After my first day of freedom from the endotracheal tube my voice normalized and I was able to ask questions and to confide in loved ones. One evening I emotionally told Kathy of my death experience. I realized after telling such a secret that I had become aware of the essence of human life and the driving force we are given to cling to this gift of life. I meditated on this natural mystery and realized that I had been given evidence of life after death, yet still clung to human life. This is the foundation of the gift of human life; that we live it to its absolute completion. I spoke with my Franciscan friar about my experience and requested a theological explanation regarding the role that The Blessed Virgin Mary played. His answer was profoundly simple. In the prayer we as Catholics say frequently, the "Hail Mary", we ask in the final verse." Holy Mary mother of God pray for us sinners now and *at the hour of our death.* "I had no need for further explanation!

Days turned into weeks and Big Bertha was retired in favor of a machine no larger than a carry-on suitcase with wheels. Of course there was always the matter of the five foot hose that did not allow me to tuck in a shirt, the long cord, the ever present batteries and their need for recharging. The inability to shower or get the LVAD wet was additional weight to carry. Soon I began to realize that my suffering was not over and this was a cross to share with Jesus.

I was listed for transplant and number one on the waiting list for my blood type, before I left the hospital. I hoped that my wait would be short. Getting into the SUV to go home was a lesson in humility. I had to ride in the back seat. I depended on other people to lift and place the machine that held my body and soul together into the back seat with me. The problem was one of engineering and my vulnerability was magnified by the way I felt faint when there was the slightest crimp in the tubing as the LVAD driver was positioned next to me. The dependency, more and more apparent with each passing day was like a raw nerve being pressed each time.

I could never get away from the machine. I started a walking program and dragged it behind me everywhere I went. People would stop and stare and I learned how it must be to always have a visible handicap. I would roll it down sidewalks and police cars would stop when they saw the five foot hose and roll by slowly sizing up whether or not I was a terrorist of some sort. I never went unnoticed and could never just be part of the background. At the end of my daily three mile walk I would retreat to my apartment, under the watchful eye of my wife for the rest of the 24 hours each day.

There were three failures requiring switching to the backup. The first was a nightmare come true. I stood paralyzed looking at the digital warning of impending disaster while Kathy ran to get the backup machine. I was literally soaked in sweat from the adrenaline surge and the fear as she fumbled with the tube trying to make the transfer back to safety. It seemed like forever as I watched her shaking hands change the connections. Relief came with the cessation of the warning sirens and the resumption of the metronome pounding of the backup as it surged into action. I endured the entire episode without loss of consciousness.

The next time a backup battery alarm sounded and another switch of machines had to be performed. This time with less fear I stood watching Kathy perform the transfer and fainted when I was disconnected. No surge of adrenaline kept my blood pressure high enough to maintain consciousness. I realized that my confidence in Kathy's ability to help me change devices was no substitute for following the rules. The third time I had a failure I lay patiently on a bed during the transfer. Even then the lightheadedness came back. I began to think of my machine as a cross to carry and the mechanical failures as falls. Jesus fell three times on his way to Calvary. I would meditate on this as I walked my 3 miles every day.

In addition to meditation I was getting very weary of carrying the LVAD with me. I spent my time in prayer asking God to bring an end to this part of my suffering. Time was marching onward and I seemed no closer to the end. One day while walking and lugging my "cross" with me I offered a prayer for the intercession of St. Theresa asking, no pleading for God to send me a new heart by Christmas. After that prayer, on the same route I always took, there was an obstruction on the road necessitating that I turn north a block shorter than my customary route. I walked two blocks north. It was November now and I came upon a rose garden in full bloom. St. Theresa had sent me a sign of roses and my spirit was lifted with the belief that my prayers would be answered.

My doctors rejected 23 hearts as being inadequate for me and time now was painfully crawling by. Christmas arrived and the family celebrated my ability to be there with them after the events of 2008. Christmas night I got a call from RUSH. The transplant coordinator informed me that there was a heart for me in Maryland and that I should go to the hospital at 6 AM. I was there on time and the doctors and nurses made preparations. Just as the nurse began to introduce a central IV line the surgeon ran into the room and ordered them to stop. The weather made it impossible to guarantee a safe flight out for the harvesting team and impossible to be certain of a return flight. Four hours was the maximum cold ischemic time a transplant heart could survive and still function. (Cold ischemia is defined as the time the donor heart spends packed in ice after it is harvested from the donor.) We packed and returned home saddened by the loss of opportunity and a bit disappointed in the answer to my prayers.

Ten days later on the feast of the Epiphany I got another call this time, the heart came and I was transplanted. The feast of the Epiphany is the first gift giving celebration of Christmas. Indeed, I believe the Lord has a sense of humor!

Eight months have elapsed since my transplant as I finish this part of my writing. I am full of joy and peace. I search for opportunities to serve the Lord and believe He spared me for a special reason. Perhaps His intention was that I become vocal about the gift of life, He has given us. It is to be cherished and lived to its fullest and for as long as the gift lasts. Humanity is special in God's plan and life is to be held Sacred.

Postscript

Months after I started my new life with my new heart I was strong enough to go to my grandson Phil's Kindergarten class and meet the little ones who, I was told prayed daily for me at Transfiguration Grammar School in Wauconda, Illinois. I was welcomed warmly into the class and met all forty of the 6 year olds, in Mrs. James Jedd's Class. As I watched the proceedings of this marvelous teacher in a modern day Catholic grade school I recalled my days in Sister Mary Daniel's class at Our Lady of Fatima. There, on an easel, was a similar poster board with a drawing of St. Michael the Arc Angel. Each opportunity to teach was focused by Mrs. Jedd on the traditional Catholic values I recognized from my childhood. The children were joyful and well behaved and she referred to each of them as apostles or God's children as she conducted the class. I, of course was there for "Show and Tell'. One brave little girl asked me if they let me bring my old heart home with me?

I smiled at the question and politely said no. Since them I have meditated in wonderment about the concept of "heart" as we come to understand the symbolism of what it represents. It represents life, spirit, belief, courage, commitment, personhood, perseverance, truth, values, and most of all love. And the answer I should have given to that little girl was "yes"!

I had never foreseen the need for writing this dedication until late in the progress of this book. In the beginning of the Rosary we pray three Hail Mary's and they are intended for Faith, Hope and Charity. As I conclude, I will share with you the essence of how I use this part of my prayer life every day. I pray the first Hail Mary for Faith and dedicate it to the memory of the work done by Sr. Mary Daniel planting the seeds of faith in myself and so many others. The second Hail Mary is for Mrs Jedd and the Transfiguration grammar school that they will continue their unselfish mission to teach the faith to all those young people in their school and that that faith will grow in them and continue to expand. It gave me hope to experience that visit. The third Hail Mary is for Charity which is Love. The dedication in love is for all of my friends in the Lord especially Andy Zovko and all of those who are influenced by those friends even those who are yet only touched by silent prayer that they will receive God's Grace.

I will exalt you, O Lord
For you lifted me out of the depths
And did not let my enemies gloat over me.

O Lord, my God, I called to you for help
And you healed me.
Psalm 30 1-19

The things that Thou Hast Seen

I n revelations 1-19 John wrote, "The revelation of Jesus Christ, which God gave him to show his servants what must soon take place. He made it known by sending his angel to his servant John, **2**who testifies to everything he saw—that is, the word of God and the testimony of Jesus Christ. **3**Blessed is the one who reads the words of this prophecy, and blessed are those who hear it and take to heart what is written in it, because the time is near.

He further wrote what he was told, ""Write, therefore, what you have seen, what is now and what will take place later"..............."

In the time that has passed by since I made my physical recovery I am faced with continued evidence of God's hand in my life and others. I have traveled farther spiritually than I ever imagined I would. Physically I have my post-transplant trials and tribulations. Sixteen heart biopsies in the first twelve months and multiple frustrations with side effects of medications and my new companions hypertension, hypercholesterolemia and antirejection drugs have forced me to keep the faith with my doctor's plans. As a result I have thrived. My motive to write this end to my reflections is not based on a sense that I am called to be a Prophet like John. Rather I am called to be a witness to the Spirit in the world today as was John in his day. When the Spirit asks for an expectation of performance, there is no debate. Thus I continue with pen in hand to write for you what the Lord has allowed me to know.

In Paul's second letter to the Philippians it is stated. "Wherefore God also hath highly exalted him, and hath given him a name which is above every name, That at the name of Jesus every knee might bow, of those in heaven, and those on earth, and those under the earth; And every tongue might confess, that Jesus Christ is Lord to the glory of God the Father."

I have considered the occasion when the Spirit commanded, instead of asked me to "Call Mary." People have asked, "What was that like? Did I hear a voice? Did I see God?" Calling to mind the scriptural reference to the exaltation of the Lord, that "all Knees will bend to the Lord" I can say this is an excellent way to explain a command from God. When He reveals Himself and gives a command there is no way to resist it. His Will shall be done!

Epilogue 2012

*T*he Gospa
I recently celebrated Mother's Day, here in United States, May 13th 2012. Where I had a speaking engagement at the University of Notre Dame in Indiana. I was scheduled to speak at the National Medjugorje Conference. It was On the day prior to my speech, as I sat in the main Church contemplating the meaning of Motherhood, that Fr. Bill Zavaski read the Gospel of St.John for that particular day.

"As the Father has loved Me so I have loved you.

Remain in my love, If you keep my commandments, you will remain in my love,

Just as I have kept my father's commandments and remain in his love.

I have told you this so that my own joy may be in you and your joy is complete.

This is my commandment: love one another as I have loved you.

A man can have no greater love than to lay down his life for his friends.

You are my friends, if you do what I command you.

I shall not call you servants anymore, because a servant does not know his masters business;

I call you friends, because I have made known to you everything I have learnt from my Father.

You did not choose me, no, I chose you;

And I commissioned you to go out and bear fruit, fruit that will last; and then the Father will give you anything you ask him in my name.

What I command you, is to love one another." John 15; 9-17

Following this most powerful reading of God's word, our pastor Fr. Bill Zavasky began a homily explaining this commandment of love and weaving into it the understanding of a mother's love for her children and the need to extend our understanding of the concept of mother to all those in our life that nurture us in one way or another. The command to love came from God and the understanding of love and nurturing in motherhood side by side brought into sharp focus the understanding of Jesus' love for His mother Mary.

When he was on the Cross just before the end He spoke to Mary his mother in John's presence and declared 'Woman behold thy son" This was not a reference to Himself nailed to a cross but a giving symbolically to John and therefore the rest of us Mary as our mother. He followed this by saying "Son behold your Mother."

This is an excellent example of how one needs to read scripture in context and not take one isolated verse of scripture and give it a different meaning than was originally intended.

It is said that, when John Paul II was shot in attempted assassination, the words he spoke were beseeching mother Mary to come now. Shortly after this event the apparitions began in

Medjugorje, Yugoslavia. I have come to believe that this gathering of people from all over the world, is definitely important in our time, if we are to have peace. Mary's frequent visits to people in worldly apparitions is associated constantly with this theme of Motherhood.

At Guadalupe Mary said to Juan Diego, "Am I not here, who am your Mother?" And then at Medjugorje, Our lady said, "Little children, do not forget that I am your Mother." These messages and the connections that I have perceived between Christians and Catholics even Jews and Muslims all seem to indicate some sense of gathering good faithful people back to God in these secular divided times of our lives. I would go so far as to call this time the great gathering.

The phone call from Lou the Jew

When I first came back from Medjugorje I was truly born again and filled with the joy of Christian Hope, Love and Faith. I began to tell anyone who would listen, about my experiences there, and the word soon went out that I was a changed man.

I was certainly well informed about the events that surrounded Mary's apparitions in Medjugorje. One after noon I received a phone call from Lou and Jill Avon. Lou a stranger to me, was a Jew who had heard of the apparitions at Medjugorje. He and his wife were considering making a trip to Medjugorje in an effort to find spiritual peace after the accidental death of their son. It seemed that Lou and Jill were both cultural Jews and not very religious. They were passionately seeking something that I could only understand as mystical. They also explained why they needed to know from me if they should go to Medjugorje. I did my fair share of talking on the phone with them that afternoon. I believe I helped them at least know what to expect once they got there. Theirs is an interesting story that is filled with many coincidences related to what I see as a gathering of souls toward God with Mary, Our Spiritual Mother, leading the way.

Here is the whole story as I remember it:

Their son was killed in an accident just before Christmas. His mother was in a state of collapse and was inconsolable. She was unable to eat or sleep without medical assistance. She also needed to be sedated. One night, she finally did get to sleep but was awakened just before 1 a.m. by what she described as a beautiful lady, who told her to go downstairs and turn on the television to a certain channel, which happened to be the Catholic one of EWTN. She apparently turned on the video recording also. By the time she got to turn the television the program was already in progress. It was a priest talking about suffering. He had already mentioned different types of suffering but by the time the screen showed the program the priest was pointing at the camera saying, "This is for a mother who lost a son" Whatever the priest said on the screen that morning, spoke deeply to her mother's heart and she knew that the message was for her. She no longer needed sedation nor sleeping aids and was completely at peace. Lou was amazed and asked her what had caused the change in her. He too was at peace and curious to know more about this priest on EWTN.

Several weeks passed as they both industriously tuned in to EWTN to find this same priest who had several different spots on the Network at that time. One night he happened to be speaking about Medjugorje and the program opened with a picture of Our Lady of Medjugorje. The Mother was excited as she shouted, that is the lady who woke me and told me to turn on the TV. This led them to seeking me out since they had also heard from somebody about a doctor who had been there and was a converted agnostic. This is not the end of the coincidences but first of many more.

"Trust Him"

Events of life sometimes lead us to surprising relationships with people we might not have ever met. I was on an airplane riding in First Class from Chicago O'Hare to Detroit Michigan. I was on route to an assembly of investors in a Laser Hair Removal chain. We were about to be courted by the Major partners in response to an additional private offering of shares in the already successful company that had ambitious plans to expand.

Doctors are usually targets of all sorts of investment schemes throughout their professional lives. I had become a partner in the company almost against my will because of the persuasive power of Benn Gilmore my best almost lifelong friend. Benn was once an atheist who told me that if he was in a crashing plane "I would pray not to pray" He just did not believe. Over the years through many peoples prayers and patient storming of Heaven Benn was born again and now was a committed Christian man. He talked me into this investment for which I am forever grateful and it was he who personally vetted each investor based on their strength of character and moral standards. So it happened that sitting on the plane in the seat next to me was Wafik Hanna MD. Wafik is a Coptic Catholic from Egypt and he specializes in cosmetic surgery and has celebrity status in the Chicago Suburbs. We spent the conference getting to know one another and became fast friends in the Lord as well as through the mutual investment and his very professional approach to his specialty.

Long before I was in end stage heart failure Wafik was a friend and even provided some minor medical attention to my wife Kathy related to a skin cancer on her ear. When I was in the hospital on the artificial heart (LVAD) she left one day when things were still not settled. His office was on her way home and she stopped in to the office to bring him up to date and broke into sobs and tears. Wafik stopped his busy schedule and spent time counseling her spiritually. She told me that his last words to her that day were, "Remember what I said, Trust in the Lord". She left feeling consoled and remembered stopping to stare at the infant of Prague Statue that Wafik kept in his office. On the way home she tapped into Dr. Hanna's devotion to the Infant of Prague and said a prayer for my recovery and that I would survive to get a transplant. While on the highway a large Black car passed her and abruptly pulled in front of her. She noted the vanity plate on the car said "Trst Him" in the seven letters allowed by Illinois. Just then an ambulance blew her doors off rushing past her on the highway. Letters on the vehicle said "Organ Transplant Vehicle" Tears left her eyes and she continued home with renewed faith that the prayer assault on heaven was being heard.

I have since recovering used the same approach to my patients as my friend Wafik did with Kathy. When all seems lost, you think you have reached the bottom, Trust Him.

In the days since then and considering all that I have had the fortune to experience even the misfortune to endure I have often thought, "Why me?" And frankly I don't know the answer to that mystery. I am back to work full time and working on challenging projects in medicine that I would have never dreamed of before some of these events swept me up and tempered me like steel.

Perhaps is all of this is part of God's plan. I remain here to accomplish something. I don't know what, but I keep listening for and searching for clues to the mystery. Perhaps I supposed to recount this story to you the reader. To tell the tale of how I came back into the Light of God. Perhaps I am here to continue the original plan I made involving helping others through the medical arts. I have certainly become a better doctor .I don't announce this from pride, I simply repeat to you the reports I hear from patients that I tend who tell me I have made a difference for them.

There are great changes going on in our world. Certainly politics aside the climate is changing and will if it continues change the inhabitants of this planet. War is prolific and life is held in *cheap disregard. Human rights are violated and there are few people left with the credentials to make the argument that there should be fundamental rights. Population control by government rule in China is no less moral than the willful destruction of the unborn by the "right to choose" in America.*

The financial crises in our world are pitting the rich against the poor at an alarming rate. Governments are falling like dominoes in the Middle East. Israel is threatened with extinction. The west is threatened too many ways to recount it this memoir. Humanity has lost not gained ground in all this. No one really knows what is next. It seems to me everywhere I go people are looking for something else. Something that is lost in the modern world. They fill their lives in this quest for being fulfilled and at peace with multiple diverse endeavors most secular many holy. They are listening for something, some elusive answer. Some as they gather together begin to see clearly that without the Lord we are really powerless.

I keep listening. I am no longer arrogant enough to announce my plans to God. I have done that dozens of times. In a sense, I have learned how to make God laugh.

I am glad to be back and useful. I plan to spend the rest of my days in service to God and his creation. I hope when it is time to experience God's laugh in paradise.

Made in the USA
Lexington, KY
06 February 2018